Praise for *The Remote Facilitator's Pocket Guide*

"We are all woefully unprepared for the evolution of effective spaces into the distributed environment. This book teaches us what to do so that we need not be."
—**Aveshan Govender, Engineering Manager, Spotify**

"This is inclusive design at its finest: an invitation to go beyond our ordinary context and be involved in the discovery along the way. I have an increasing demand for distributed facilitation, and this approach is the best I've ever experienced."
—**Cara Turner, CEO, Project codeX**

"This groundbreaking book is for people who want remote connections to be at least as productive, vibrant, and alive as the very best gatherings with everyone in the same room. It's delightfully refreshing for experts and also offers a fresh, safe, inspiring start point for anyone new to facilitation of any kind."
—**Steve Holyer, Agile Coach and Facilitator, CoachingCocktails.com**

"Remote meetings can't be considered cutting edge anymore—yet we are surprisingly bad at them. Kirsten and Jay-Allen understand how people behave in meetings and how you can encourage them to have positive behaviors that lead to vastly more effective meetings. Their art is a mix of psychology, empathy, and practical techniques."
—**Ted Pietrzak, Vice President, Application Modernization, The Charles Schwab Corporation**

"Jay-Allen and Kirsten provide loads of practical ideas to experiment with to make your meetings more productive, equal, and fun. If you care about your teams, your effectiveness, and your general well-being at remote work, this book is for you!"
—**Louise Perold, Quality Manager**

THE REMOTE FACILITATOR'S POCKET GUIDE

Date: 8/4/20

THE REMOTE FACILITATOR'S POCKET GUIDE

Kirsten Clacey
and Jay-Allen Morris

BK

Berrett–Koehler Publishers, Inc.

Berrett-Koehler Publishers, Inc.
1333 Broadway, Suite 1000
Oakland, CA 94612-1921
Tel: (510) 817-2277
Fax: (510) 817-2278
www.bkconnection.com

ORDERING INFORMATION

Quantity sales. Special discounts are available on quantity purchases by corporations, associations, and others. For details, contact the "Special Sales Department" at the Berrett-Koehler address above.

Individual sales. Berrett-Koehler publications are available through most bookstores. They can also be ordered directly from Berrett-Koehler: Tel: (800) 929-2929; Fax: (802) 864-7626; www.bkconnection.com.

Orders for college textbook / course adoption use. Please contact Berrett-Koehler: Tel: (800) 929-2929; Fax: (802) 864-7626.

Distributed to the U.S. trade and internationally by Penguin Random House Publisher Services.

Berrett-Koehler and the BK logo are registered trademarks of Berrett-Koehler Publishers, Inc.

Printed in the United States of America

Berrett-Koehler books are printed on long-lasting acid-free paper. When it is available, we choose paper that has been manufactured by environmentally responsible processes. These may include using trees grown in sustainable forests, incorporating recycled paper, minimizing chlorine in bleaching, or recycling the energy produced at the paper mill.

Library of Congress Cataloging-in-Publication Data

Names: Clacey, Kirsten, author. | Morris, Jay-Allen, author.
Title: The remote facilitator's pocket guide / Kirsten Clacey and Jay-Allen Morris.
Description: First edition. | Oakland, CA : Berrett-Koehler Publishers, [2020] | Includes bibliographical references and index.
Identifiers: LCCN 2020003197 | ISBN 9781523089109 (paperback) | ISBN 9781523089116 (pdf) | ISBN 9781523089123 (epub)
Subjects: LCSH: Videoconferencing. | Group facilitation. | Virtual work teams. | Virtual reality in management.
Classification: LCC HF5734.7 .C533 2020 | DDC 658.4/56–dc23
LC record available at https://lccn.loc.gov/2020003197

First Edition
26 25 24 23 22 21 20   10 9 8 7 6 5 4 3 2 1

Book producer: Westchester Publishing Company
Cover design and illustration: Yvonne Chan
Interior illustrations: Kirsten Clacey

*To our teams who experimented with us,
and Nelson and Wesley
who supported us throughout.*

CONTENTS

FOREWORD BY ESTHER DERBY   *ix*

INTRODUCTION   1

WHY IS REMOTE COLLABORATION DIFFICULT?   7

WHAT IS THE ROLE OF A (REMOTE) FACILITATOR?   20

PRINCIPLE 1: CREATE EQUAL OPPORTUNITY   28

PRINCIPLE 2: ENABLE FLOW   48

PRINCIPLE 3: GUIDE WITH VISUALS   62

PRINCIPLE 4: NURTURE CONNECTION   77

PRINCIPLE 5: ENABLE PLAYFUL LEARNING   90

PRINCIPLE 6: MASTER YOUR TOOLS   105

AFTER THE CALL: HOW TO MAINTAIN
CONNECTION WHEN THE CALL ENDS   115

TYING IT TOGETHER   122

NOTES   *147*
ACKNOWLEDGMENTS   *151*
INDEX   *155*
ABOUT THE AUTHORS   *161*

FOREWORD

I spent years honing my facilitation skills. I learned how people process information. I learned how to create an environment that enables groups to share information, discuss, think, and decide together. I then introduced a process for helping groups do just that, detailed in *Agile Retrospectives: Making Good Teams Great* (2006). That book describes how teams can reflect, learn, and improve—when they are together.

However, remote meetings are a different animal. Over the years, I've adapted practices and come up with workarounds for remote meetings. Still, remote meetings often don't have the oomph of in-person interactions.

As a participant, I've spent countless hours in remote meetings. While I am certain it hasn't actually been an eternity, sometimes it feels that way. Faced with low participation, isolation, and lack of feedback, sometimes I check out. I'm not alone. People often take refuge in online solitaire, checking email, Twitter, Slack, or doing "real" work. Even when the tools allow for visual communication and screen sharing, the default is camera off—which makes it easier to disengage and hide out. It doesn't feel like robust collaboration, no matter how much the participants and leaders wish it were so. Perhaps you've had this experience, too.

It doesn't have to be this way.

I had the pleasure to meet Jay-Allen and Kirsten at the Regional Scrum Gathering in Durban, South Africa in 2018. Their topic, "Hacking Remote Facilitation," intrigued me. I figured that while I knew some things, it couldn't hurt to see what other people were doing. I might pick up a tip or two.

Their session provided the best advice on the mechanics of remote facilitation I've seen. Anywhere.

Their lovely new book describes in detail how to make remote meetings more participative, engaging, and useful. It also makes clear that their ideas go deeper than mere mechanics.

Jay-Allen and Kirsten developed their methods based on a true appreciation for creating space for people to collaborate. Their values and experience show up in the six principles outlined in the book. The methods that implement each principle derive from the science of how our brains function. Throughout the book, an understanding of what people need to collaborate effectively shines though.

Jay-Allen and Kirsten don't just tell you what to do. They explain *why* the methods work. After studying this book, you will have a starting set of methods. You'll also gain the knowledge to adapt, modify, and create your own methods to fit your context.

Collaboration is the heart of creative work. But collaborative work isn't always easy. Collaborative work requires hearing and harmonizing different viewpoints, harnessing constructive conflict, and reaching decisions that a group will own. Groups struggle through, sometimes with damaged relationships to uncertain results, even when they are face-to-face. Remoteness exacerbates the issue.

This costs organizations in wasted time and wasted money. Worse, the failure to overcome the challenge of remote collaboration drains engagement. People check out during meetings, and often stay checked out. People who might come up with creative solutions and market-changing innovation never feel the spark.

Collaboration and creativity across distance isn't out of reach. Remote meetings can be engaging and productive. This book will show you how.

Esther Derby
Duluth, MN

INTRODUCTION

Everyone is on mute.

Your heart is pounding; you are not usually this nervous in meetings.

What were you saying?

The energy on the call feels like it is slipping away.

Very few people speak.

You hoped this meeting would be more engaging than the last one.

It isn't.

If the above scene feels at all familiar, we can relate. When remote meetings go badly, they go really badly. Few things feel as lonely and intimidating as speaking to a screen, with unreadable faces staring back in silence. We wrote this book to help you improve the quality of your remote meetings. With a little awareness, some planning, and some practice, you can make your remote meetings effective, engaging, and a powerful mechanism for collaboration within your organization.

We hope this book enables you to think differently about your remote meetings and find new inspiration. We hope that you feel a little braver in remote meetings. That when you finish reading you have something practical that makes your meetings more productive. That your teams enjoy remote meetings a little bit more. That your meetings achieve more powerful outcomes. That your organization begins to reap the fruit of meaningful meetings. We hope that the growing trend of remote working is made healthier by the work of this book.

WHY CARE ABOUT REMOTE MEETINGS?

Organizations are built on tons of interactions and decisions, both big and small. From a few people compiling a report, to a big group deciding the budgeting strategy for a high-risk project, these moments of people thinking together combine and compound to create the complex ecosystem that is a company. If we explore this a bit further, meetings are possibly one of the smallest and most discrete units of collaboration within organizations. Meetings are also one of the most impacted spaces in distributed environments.

While 10 years ago, remote working and distributed teams might have been considered "cutting edge," current trends indicate that this style of working is becoming the norm for many organizations. Multiple-location offices, a shift in work-life balance, regional skills scarcity, and city congestion are but a few drivers of this global trend.[1] However, many teams and organizations are battling to reach the same degree of effectiveness and satisfaction in their remote spaces.[2] We believe it is possible to drastically improve an organization's outcomes by focusing on the quality of its remote meetings.

WHO IS THIS BOOK FOR?

We wrote this book for anyone seeking to get more value from remote meetings, whether you're a seasoned facilitator, a new facilitator, or someone hoping to improve team meetings. As we detangle the complexity of remote collaboration, the actions of the facilitator will be the primary focus. By zooming in on this role and specifically the opportunity that skillful remote facilitation brings, facilitators/leaders/team members will be empowered with principles and actionable methods to enhance their organization's effectiveness.

For those who have never encountered facilitation as a craft before or used it as a mechanism to improve meeting outcomes and effectiveness, this book introduces the topic and includes a lightweight introduction to the basics. We'll make facilitation accessible and take you on a journey of going deeper in your understanding. We will connect facilitation, organizational effectiveness, and remote working.

HOW CAN YOU USE THIS BOOK?

At times this may look a lot like a general facilitation book, and if it helps you to improve in-person facilitation, then we are really happy. We know that some of the content is equally relevant to in-person meetings, but we chose to include it when we felt it was *especially* relevant in remote meetings. So, bear with us if at times you think that what we are saying relates to in-person meetings.

To move beyond a theoretical understanding, we have added a set of questions at the end of each chapter; we hope that you allow yourself some time with them. Facilitation is both an art and a science and so we encourage you to seek opportunities to practice and receive feedback. If you are new to facilitation, you may find the chapter on "What is the Role of a (Remote) Facilitator?" particularly useful. We encourage you to also do a little self-exploration into the world of facilitation to supplement what you learn here.

A few disciplines have been combined in this book, particularly social psychology, neuroscience, and facilitation. Despite the theoretical background, we want this book to be practical and actionable. Each chapter has distinct sections that you can flip to for reference or skip if you want to get to the practical stuff. Chapters follow a similar structure.

Each chapter begins with a metaphor to make abstract concepts relatable. We then deep-dive into theory around the principle, often guided by illustrative stories from our experience. We believe a basic understanding of how the brain works is incredibly helpful in navigating social spaces and so each chapter has a section titled "Under the Hood." These sections discuss neuroscientific research and its relevance to remote meetings. Finally, each chapter concludes with some practical ideas on mechanics and methods for you to begin experimenting with as well as questions to help you integrate what you have learned. As you work through this book, we invite you to invest some time reflecting on the questions we pose, to challenge some of your thinking and to arrive at deeper understandings of these spaces.

Although this book is intended to be a practical tool, we take a principles-based approach to remote facilitation. All tools and methods are only as impactful as the skill with which they are wielded. We believe that in exploring the principles behind the methods, you will gain a deeper understanding of remote facilitation and become a wiser steward of these spaces. Tools in and of themselves have no power—the power and outcome (positive or negative) depends entirely on their application.

Finally, we'd like to note that no two meetings are the same; all have differing audiences and purposes. A meeting of senior executives requires something different from a facilitator than a team meeting that happens regularly. While different meetings require different strategies, it is difficult to draw clear distinctions between them. Just because there is a senior audience does not mean the meeting will necessarily be a certain way. As such, this book covers a broad range of strategies and will encourage you to use your intuition to decide what is applicable to your specific context. We encourage you to experiment with one technique at a time, seek feedback often, and be transparent when you are experimenting.

WHO ARE WE?

We first approached remote facilitation with an experimental mindset due to the changing needs of our organization at the time. Global expansion had led to multiple office locations and industry trends were putting increasing pressure on "remote working" being offered as a benefit to staff. Working as organizational facilitators and team coaches, we were tasked with guiding the company through this transition. One of our main goals was to make remote meetings as human and effective as our in-person ones, maintaining productive collaboration through this transition. We're grateful that we were given the space to explore and experiment from the start.

We have since spent years studying what makes remote interactions different, looking for answers in neuroscience (What's happening in our brains when we look at someone through a screen?), social psychology (How do group dynamics play out in the absence of co-location?), Agile (How do we prioritize people and interactions when we cannot see people?), and facilitation (What can facilitation teach us about navigating complexity?). We now specialize in enabling distributed teams to reach high performance by using a combination of adapted facilitation techniques, team coaching methods, and Agile frameworks. We speak at conferences, host workshops, consult with teams and organizations, and have founded an online learning community of international remote facilitators. We are passionate about advancing the craft of remote facilitation and enabling organizations to thrive in the absence of co-location.

WHY IS REMOTE
COLLABORATION DIFFICULT?

---

*"Vulnerability is hard and it's scary
and it feels dangerous."*

—Brené Brown[3]

When we think about meetings, *vulnerability* is one of the first words that come to mind. Brené Brown defines vulnerability as, "Uncertainty, risk and emotional exposure."[4] As you walk into a meeting, outcomes can be uncertain, the process for achieving them may be unclear, and, if you're really attached to the outcomes, there is a degree of emotional exposure you will probably endure to defend what you value.

Meetings are one of the most common mechanisms for collaboration, and they house immense potential for organizations. High-quality meetings directly influence an organization's ability to achieve its outcomes. At the same time, meetings have the potential to be profoundly vulnerable spaces. Perhaps this is one of the main reasons that so many people struggle with remote meetings: a cocktail of factors, such as technical barriers and invisible group norms, increase the uncertainty and risk in an already vulnerable space. In this chapter, we highlight three stories that illustrate some of the most common challenges of remote meetings. We also look at a model from neuroscience of how human beings perceive threat in social situations. How we solve these challenges will be the work of the remaining chapters.

THE STORY OF A CO-LOCATED TEAM THAT TRIED REMOTE WORKING

We facilitated a co-located software engineering team working on their company's core back-end technology. The team had the autonomy to choose how they worked. One of the decisions they made was to work from home one day a week because most team members had long commutes.

The team's in-person meetings flowed; despite two individuals being more outspoken, differing opinions were voiced and heard. Lighthearted comments were passed and more often than not, outcomes that the team believed in were reached . . . except on remote days. The same team in a remote setting often lost their sense of humor, and despite desires to be otherwise, found themselves in meetings that often felt tense and awkward, with the two more dominant voices occupying a lot more airtime than usual. The team was frustrated that their remote meetings felt less engaging and a lot more draining.

Some of the above might sound familiar. Perhaps you have witnessed dynamics shift in a remote space. Despite the trust built over the team's two years of working together and their shared commitment to succeeding with remote work, remote meetings were difficult.

As we explored how to improve these meetings, the challenges we were experiencing became clearer:

- **Group norms are invisible:** While it is easy to replace explicit norms, the implicit norms that guide behavior are difficult to identify. For example, it is usually quite easy to sense if someone would like to speak if you see them breathe in, lean forward, or raise their hand. Even if the group reestablishes new remote norms and chooses to keep their videos on or use a "raise hand" mechanism, the experience is not the same. As social beings, a lot of our interactions are guided by intuition rather than overt rules. Replacing all the subtleties that help us navigate social interactions is really difficult.

- **Overreliance on verbal communication:** In the co-located meetings, the team would mix their communication styles by speaking, using sticky notes, or writing on the physical board. Unintentionally, this subtle action provided alternative communication mechanisms and leveled the playing field for different kinds of thinkers. People who needed time to think before speaking (typically the more introverted team members) were able to write their thoughts down. Contrasted with the remote calls in which 100 percent of the communication was often verbal, some people experienced the space as significantly more stressful. The absence of visuals can often result in biases towards certain kinds of thinking.

- **Technical barriers break flow:** Each time someone missed something that was said, asked for it to be repeated—or, worse, gave up trying to hear—the flow and focus of the meeting changed. With each interruption, frustration rose.

■ **Communication takes additional effort:** To convey an idea in person, participants could draw on a whiteboard or use hand gestures to provide additional information that might be difficult to convey with words. To do so was relatively easy and quick. The team lost this ease of communication because they had to seek and prepare alternative tools, which felt less fluid and accessible.

The small things we overlooked and took for granted in person became more obvious in a remote space. The change in environment changed behavior. If unaddressed, that change could have led to the formation of unhealthy behaviors and mindsets about meetings.

UNDER THE HOOD
USING NEUROSCIENCE TO MAKE SENSE OF REMOTE COLLABORATION CHALLENGES

Meetings are social spaces. As such, the neuroscience of human social behavior is foundational in developing effective ways to improve them. In 2008, David Rock developed one of the most perceptive social cognition models that we have seen. His model, called SCARF, is built on the idea that the brain is primed to avoid threat and move toward reward, with the default being identifying and reacting to perceived threats. His research shows that unless we intentionally create conditions that enable the brain to perceive the situation positively, it is likely that we will see the negative first.

SCARF[5] is an acronym for the five primary needs of the brain from which a person may perceive threat or reward. We believe these are helpful lenses for understanding the challenges we experience in remote spaces. Each person in a meeting has a different combination of these needs and we have found that remote spaces complicate their fulfillment. We'll describe the five domains below and reference them in the coming chapters:

1. **Status**: How important or valued do you feel? If you feel undervalued or underappreciated, you are less likely to bring your best self to a meeting space, because your brain responds to the perceived threat. If we think about a remote meeting in which someone speaks but the group continues talking over that person, they can feel excluded. While a technical glitch could have caused the issue, this person is now feeling less valued, which impacts how they will engage in the meeting.

2. **Certainty**: How much clarity is there in a given situation? For people with a high need for certainty, the absence of information in a given situation can lead to creating false stories, which usually are negative (our brain's default). For example, we might tell ourselves that the reason they did not tell us that information was

because they did not want our team to know—whereas in reality they may simply have forgotten to tell us. If we think about the invisible group norms in remote meetings, this lack of clarity and certainty can feel quite scary for some. How does one engage in a remote meeting? As we wait for people to join, the ambiguity of not knowing how to act in this space can lead to feelings of vulnerability.

3. **Autonomy**: How much control do you feel you have in a given situation? Without some degree of choice, we can feel out of control, which can be perceived as very threatening by some. If we think about a remote meeting that overemphasizes verbal communication, it is possible that different kinds of thinkers may feel less control in this situation and begin to feel threatened and/or withdrawn/disengaged if the space does not allow for their contribution as easily.

4. **Relatedness**: How connected and close do you feel to those around you? Not feeling a part of something or being excluded from the "in-group" can be experienced as incredibly painful for some. As group norms are made invisible in remote spaces, feeling connected and close to those around us is less likely. For people with a high need for connectedness, the meeting space can become a lot more vulnerable.

5. **Fairness**: How balanced and equal does a given situation feel? You might receive a bonus with which you are really happy, until you discover that your colleague received more.[6] Perceived fairness really matters for some people. Accidentally favoring the loud voices or more confident

speakers in a remote meeting could create a perception of unfairness. Similarly, if someone is struggling with tech and gets left behind for a bit, this can feel quite unfair for some and begin to create unhelpful states in the brain.

THE STORY OF THE MEETING EVERYONE FEARED

A few years ago, we worked with a global financial technology firm that had a weekly meeting in which people across the business dialed in to discuss the top priorities for the company. Participants were spread across Africa, Europe, and Asia. The person responsible for holding the meeting did not have facilitation experience so we invite you to withhold judgment. The meeting usually began by screen-sharing a document in which numerous people had to account for the status of their project, answer any questions from the audience, and justify any delays. There were usually between 30 and 40 people on these calls. The owner of the meeting would insist that each participant turn on their video so that they could ensure everyone was paying attention.

It is relatively common for organizations to have status reporting–flavored meetings. It is also not uncommon for these kinds of meetings to feel intimidating, unsafe, and defensive. What saddened us in these meetings went beyond these common pitfalls of reporting-style behavior. The atmosphere, regardless of the content, was more often than not tense. This tension led to unhelpful behaviors cropping up and skewed the outcomes being reached:

- People who were usually positive and engaged at work would become defensive, withdrawn, or the other extreme—aggressive.

- The information did not flow smoothly throughout the session, which led to people feeling frustrated or disengaged.

The remote environment really influenced the behavior of attendees. No one wanted the meeting to be this way and yet no one was aware of why the meeting was so.

This example illustrates four additional challenges we often observe in remote meetings:

- **Isolation exaggerates fear:** When people joined this call, they were already a little nervous (due to the reputation of this meeting). On days when there was a heated argument or a possibly hostile accusation, the feeling of being alone and separate compounded the fear. Rather than being in a room in which participants could see each other, and feel a sense of relatedness, everyone was in their own space wondering what others were thinking and feeling. This uncertainty and "separateness" compounded the fear. Thinking about SCARF, those with a high need for *Relatedness* may have particularly struggled with this.

- **Multitasking is both easy and expensive:** We see this often in remote meetings. In this particular meeting, we came to understand that about 80 percent of people on this call had other tabs open and were multitasking. Group norms tend to result in most people paying attention in in-person meetings; it's really obvious if someone starts scrolling on their phone next to you. On calls though, it's much easier to drift into another space. The result this had on the meeting was that people lost context and in turn responded with possibly inappropriate or incomplete information. These poor responses further complicated the meeting by resulting in:

- Increased frustration for other participants
- Poorer-quality outcomes
- Some people perceiving these kinds of behaviors as a threat to *Fairness*; not all participants were putting in the same effort

- **A facilitator's power is exaggerated/amplified:** Facilitators hold an intangible kind of power in a meeting. Often without question, a group will go along with the facilitator's suggestions or be more swayed by their ideas. This is why it is particularly important for a facilitator to maintain a neutral stance to enable the group to reach their own solutions. In remote spaces, we have observed that facilitators, if unaware of their wake, can have an exaggerated effect on the group. If the vulnerability of the remoteness has resulted in people feeling a bit more nervous and tentative than usual, a facilitator (or the authoritative voice in the room) is relied upon even more than in a co-located meeting. Similarly, opinions voiced by the facilitator are more likely to be adopted, possibly skewing the outcomes and silencing voices too hesitant to challenge. Depending on the person, this might be perceived as a threat to one's **Status** (the group is valuing what this person says over what I think), **Autonomy** (I don't feel like I can say and do what I want to), and **Fairness** (it upsets me that not everyone is being heard in the same way).

■ **Inability to see faces creates uncertainty:** A pattern that we observe frequently in remote meetings is that the ambiguity of the space/lack of control often leads to the emergence of more controlling behaviors. For example, someone feels "out of control" because they cannot see people's expressions or what they are doing, and in reaction to this feeling they make people turn on their videos. This impacts both individual **Autonomy** (I don't have any control over how I engage in this space) and the tone of the meeting. Being in a remote space already feels vulnerable; by using force, participants often feel more exposed. If someone feels uncomfortable in that moment, being forced to turn on their video is a direct threat to their **Autonomy,** which in turn affects their ability to think creatively going forward.

Vulnerable meetings can become especially vulnerable and scary when conducted in a remote setting. If the facilitator lacks this awareness and the methods for mitigating this feeling, the likelihood of reaching quality thinking and outcomes in remote meetings is really low. But fear not: there is hope for these kinds of spaces, which we'll share in upcoming chapters.

THE STORY OF THE FULLY REMOTE PROJECT KICKOFF

The beginning of a project plays a crucial role in setting the tone for interactions going forward. This story is about a project kickoff for a mobile technology development team spread across Europe and Kenya. The key stakeholders were in South Africa. The project was the first of its kind for the organization, entailing a lot of cross-team communication and alignment with external service providers. Upfront we knew that not everyone knew each other or had worked together before. The goal of this meeting was to ensure that everyone involved understood the goal of the project as well as what was expected from everyone throughout the project. This kickoff presented interesting challenges to creating **Fairness, Relatedness,** and **Autonomy.** See if you can spot how:

- **Not everyone spoke the same language at home:** Working with three different countries that had different first languages meant that meeting attendees did not feel equally comfortable speaking English in the session. The fact that there were 20-plus people already posed a challenge to hearing all voices. The fear of being misunderstood or sounding different made potential speakers feel that much more vulnerable. How many opinions, thoughts, and suggestions are missed if people do not feel comfortable speaking? We were also aware that participants needed time to process what was being said and make sense of it.

- **Cultural nuances impact the space:** Understanding the impact of cultural differences was crucial in creating a safe space. For one of the represented cultures, it was commonplace to have their leader speak on their behalf. This group was generally less outspoken than the other team from country Y. Another consideration was the words we chose and their implications. One mistake we made was to use the word "tribe" to describe an activity. While "tribe" is innocuous from our frame of reference, we learned that for some African cultures it has quite divisive connotations.

■ **Lack of familiarity:** Remote calls are challenging enough when everyone knows each other. Meetings can be even more daunting (for facilitators and participants) when the majority of people on the call do not know each other. A challenge we faced as facilitators during this meeting was finding a way to get participants to introduce themselves in a fun, nonthreatening way. Had we been unable to establish this trust, people might have felt less safe and wondered "Is it okay if I ask a question?" or "Will it be acceptable if I raise a concern?"

■ **What time is it again?:** If we use Cape Town as a baseline, we had participants on the call that were two hours ahead and some that were two hours behind. We had to find a time that accommodated all time zones as best as possible. The energy in the room can change if you're scheduling a session during someone's lunchtime or at the end of the day. Some organizations face far greater time zone differences. While it might not be possible to find an ideal time for everyone, awareness and acknowledgment of this can make people feel more respected.

CHAPTER SUMMARY: WHY IS REMOTE COLLABORATION DIFFICULT?

In this chapter we have touched on a few of the difficulties commonly faced when collaborating in remote meetings: frustration, withdrawal, and boredom. These symptoms can arise when a person's social needs are not met. Cultural and language barriers, uncertainty in what is expected, invisible group norms, and numerous distractions are but a few of the threats faced in remote meetings. No meeting is free of challenges, whether in person or remote. By paying attention to Status, Certainty, Autonomy, Relatedness, and Fairness, we minimize the chance that a person perceives a remote space as threatening. Having an awareness of the factors that complicate remote interactions is the first step in overcoming them.

Choose a remote meeting you held recently and pick a question to reflect on. We encourage you to write these answers somewhere so you can see how your understanding of remote facilitations deepens:

- ❏ What group norms might attendees be unable to see?

- ❏ How is verbal communication being balanced by other forms of communication?

- ❏ What impact are technical barriers having?

- ❏ How much effort is going into communicating for participants?

- ❏ How much fear is in the air?

- ❏ How much multitasking were you doing? What was the cost that you paid?

- ❏ How comfortable is everyone with the language being spoken?

- ❏ How much consideration are you paying to time zones?

- ❏ What cultural norms might you be overlooking?

- ❏ How familiar are attendees with one another?

WHAT IS THE ROLE OF A (REMOTE) FACILITATOR?

"Unless and until all members of a team have a common understanding of the problem, attempts to solve the problem are just so much wasted energy."

—Gerald M. Weinberg[7]

In South Africa, we have a curious culture around minibus taxis, the country's primary mode of transport (which usually carry 15–25 people). Most minibuses have three roles: the *Driver*, the *Gaatjie* (a slang word pronounced *gah-chee*), and the passengers. The Driver is responsible for getting from A to B as fast as possible, with as few incidents as possible (the definition of an incident being left to interpretation). The Gaatjie is responsible for getting passengers onto the taxi and making sure they know where they are going, when to get off, and how much to pay. The Gaatjie takes care of all variables unrelated to driving along the journey (this may involve dealing with unruly passengers or pacifying heated arguments). They may from time to time check in on the direction and nudge the Driver to stop based on what a passenger tells them. Ultimately, their focus is on managing the process.

Metaphors for facilitation seldom fit perfectly, but we mostly like this one because it speaks to how the role of a facilitator is to hold a space together, while the group moves toward an outcome. The facilitator is not necessarily driving, but they are also not sitting down and participating. Like the Gaatjie, the facilitator is focusing on the space, guiding interactions and ultimately enabling a group to go somewhere together. At times, this might mean that they need to cut short an argument or make a certain "rule of the space" explicit. Their actions are all directed toward making it easier for the group to be together.

Rather than controlling the content, a facilitator focuses on creating a container that enables healthy collaboration and input from the people in the room. Good facilitators care deeply about the quality of ideas and thinking. Guided by a deep faith in the group's ability, a facilitator creates and maintains the conditions that set the group up for success.

THE PHASES OF A MEETING

When thinking about how to facilitate a meeting, we think of the meeting itself in three phases, seen in figure 1. Quality meetings are usually achieved when a facilitator pays attention to each phase:

1. **Before the meeting starts:** It might be surprising to consider that facilitation actually begins before the meeting starts. This can involve meeting with stakeholders to understand expectations and objectives of the session, planning the meeting design, sending out relevant pre-reading material, and sharing an agenda

FIGURE 1: THREE PHASES OF MEETING FACILITATION

ahead of time. Our general advice for people new to this way of approaching meetings is to spend at least as long as the meeting is preparing for it and to be comfortable spending double the time if need be. This investment of your time ensures that within the meeting the entire group's time is well spent.

2. **During the session:** This phase looks at how the facilitator opens the space, introduces the agenda, guides the conversations, helps the group to think together, and closes the space by clarifying and summarizing any decisions or actions.

3. **After the session:** This phase entails the final step of closure, which can mean sending out any notes/ photos of outcomes or checking in with a participant if their needs were not met within the session.

There is so much more that could be said about facilitation, from understanding conflict patterns and conversation frameworks to the psychology of language and facilitation stances, the topic is immense. For those readers who have never encountered facilitation as a craft or thought of it as a means to improve meeting quality, we encourage you to spend some time learning about it. A foundation in facilitation will increase your impact in remote spaces.

REMOTE FACILITATION

As a facilitator in a remote setting, the essence of the role remains the same: we are responsible for creating the conditions that enable participants to contribute and collaborate. Given the invisible power that a facilitator holds, they can skew outcomes if they favor certain opinions over others. Remaining neutral and objective is an important part of creating an environment in which everyone feels comfortable in voicing their opinions. This remains the case whether a meeting is happening in person or virtually. However, in the absence of body language, dynamics between people can shift in interesting ways. The implicit power of the facilitator may appear magnified in a remote meeting, given the amplified sense of vulnerability of the space.

We understand that having dedicated facilitators is a luxury most organizations do not have. In most companies, facilitation is an activity and not a dedicated role. Neutrality is seldom possible when you find yourself participating and facilitating and that is okay. We encourage you to be mindful of your wake as you juggle the two roles within a meeting, possibly explaining this dichotomy up front.

Trust in the Group's Ability to Solve

Amid all the uncertainty and vulnerability that a remote space introduces, it is easy to fall into the trap of overcorrecting by controlling the space. There is a difference between being prepared and holding space in the meeting versus trying to control the details and outcomes. If you are running a brainstorming or problem-solving session, you have to believe that the group chosen to be in the space has the necessary knowledge and skills to arrive at meaningful outcomes. Overcontrolling the space will only lead to constrained/skewed outcomes.

We hold true the belief that human beings have infinite potential and the best way to bring this out is to be guided by a deep faith in a group's ability to solve, a value we observed in Antoinette Coetzee's work. There are times when more structure is required in a session to enable the group to navigate the space. However, be very critical of this inclination to control and constantly question how much you need to do and how much the group is capable of.

Guerilla Facilitation in a Remote Space

Have you ever been in a meeting that is slowly going very wrong and yet you are an attendee and so you do not know how to help? Maybe certain individuals are frequently taking the conversation off track or you get the sense that the topic being discussed is being interpreted differently by everyone. We believe it is possible to shift a meeting in a positive direction without being directly responsible for the facilitation thereof. A good friend of ours, Cara Turner, introduced us to a term we now use to describe this kind of facilitation: "guerilla facilitation." Guerilla facilitation is particularly important in remote meetings when the number of factors complicating the space are much higher than in co-located meetings.

If you begin to notice certain patterns, reflecting these back to the group can create helpful inflection points that nudge the meeting back on track. For example, "I notice Louise is trying to speak but there's no sound coming through; is it just me?" Allowing the group to pause gives everyone an opportunity to refocus and become more intentional about the conversation being had.

Guerilla facilitation requires observation, curiosity, and an authentic way of asking questions that provides the group with options that were previously not available to them. By noticing and reflecting the patterns you are seeing in the conversation, you can shift the conversation. Alternatively, you can contribute in a way that you think is needed in the meeting. You can bring awareness to the time if the meeting is going off track. You can voice a confusion you're experiencing that you suspect others are too and in so doing, normalize this open, honest way of speaking. If you take what you have learned about facilitation, you have a lens to understand the dynamics you are observing and use this information to create conditions for collaboration in the moment.

Different Kinds of Meetings?

Finally, it is worth mentioning that facilitation can look very different depending on the context. One way of understanding what will be required of a facilitator is to think about:

1. **The size of the group** (Is it a small group that is relatively familiar with each other or will there be 300 people dialing on to this call across different locations?)

2. **The kind of collaboration and engagement required** (Is this purely a presentation of information, and so little engagement is required, or is the purpose of the session to generate ideas together?)

As shown in the graph in figure 2, different facilitator actions will be required in different spaces. For example, presenting content often requires very little facilitation, although we still believe that awareness of facilitation will improve the quality of these meetings. The principles and techniques we discuss will be applicable to a variety of contexts and we leave it to you to choose which are appropriate for the spaces you find yourself in.

FIGURE 2: DIFFERENT MEETING TYPES

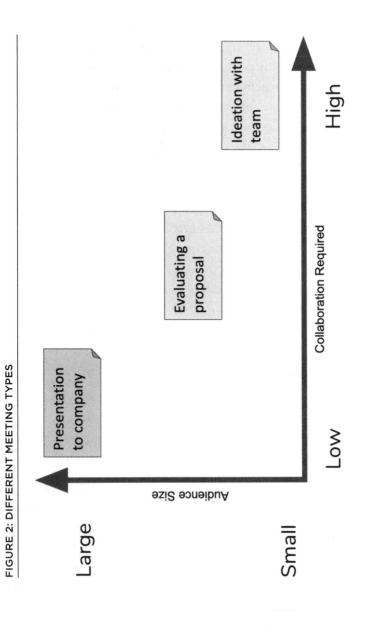

CHAPTER SUMMARY

Given the challenges of remote environments and the increased likelihood of people perceiving threat in these spaces, remote facilitation has some nuance. While the core mission remains the same, the application and focus shifts depending on the context. We looked at a framework for facilitation and how someone responsible for facilitating a meeting might approach the session: doing the necessary prework, maintaining an inclusive collaborative environment during the session, and performing any follow-up work that continues when the session ends.

The remaining chapters focus on six principles that enable a facilitator/leader/team member not only to meet the challenges of remote meetings, but to turn them into opportunities. We would like to emphasize that our focus is on remote facilitation and that it is advisable that anyone attempting to apply advanced facilitation techniques invest in understanding the foundations of facilitation.

Take some time to consider one or two of the questions below in relation to a meeting you are responsible for:

❑ How have I prepared for this session?

❑ Does everyone know what is expected of them in the meeting?

❑ How have I made it easy for participants to contribute to the meeting space?

❑ What time is it for the different attendees?

❑ How can I gauge the energy if people choose not to have their video on?

❑ How do I intend to close the space once the meeting is over?

PRINCIPLE 1:
CREATE EQUAL OPPORTUNITY

"If you aren't actively including, you're probably accidentally excluding."

—Dr. Jacqui Grey[8]

Imagine going on a safari. Picture a dirt road, sporadic potholes, some really muddy areas, and the possibility of animals approaching from any side . . . the vehicle you are in will really affect your experience. Now imagine three people setting out on safari: one person is in a beautifully kitted-out 4×4, another is in a Ferrari, and another is on a bicycle. Who do you think will have the best experience? What will the impact of the vehicle be on their experience?

When going on a safari, the vehicle is the mechanism through which passengers experience their surroundings. Similarly, in remote meetings, everyone is entering in a different context, which will result in a different experience. For people who are in the room having face-to-face conversation, it's likely their experience will be pretty smooth. For someone attending remotely, listening through a speaker and observing a whiteboard through a camera might at times feel a lot like bumping through a game reserve on a rickety bicycle. It's really difficult to enjoy the experience and contribute when the rest of the group is racing ahead in their fancy 4×4.

If someone has been invited to a meeting to solve a problem or be involved in decision making, it is important that they are able to contribute and that it is both safe and easy enough for them to do so. Who is involved in solving a problem is equally as important as how they go about doing so. We believe a condition of an effective meeting is that the right people are involved in the discussion. Hearing all voices matters. That does not necessarily mean that all meeting attendees have the same degree of authority or influence over the outcome, but as far as possible facilitators should provide the space where all people can be heard.

There are many reasons why creating an equal opportunity to contribute is important. Consider a scenario in which two individuals dominate the conversation in a meeting:

- How likely is it that the group will defend or action the outcomes outside of the meeting if they were not allowed to participate in reaching them?

- What opportunities might have been missed by not hearing some other opinions and voices?

- What might the cost to the organization be in reaching a skewed outcome?

Both team motivation and quality thinking are at risk when some voices are silenced. The inverse is equally unhelpful: no one speaks. By considering how to design and hold a meeting in which there is an equal opportunity for participation and contribution, we believe a facilitator improves the quality of outcomes.

UNDER THE HOOD
THE BRAIN AND PHYSICAL PAIN

Before we get practical and explain how you can create equal opportunity for participation, we want to go a little deeper into what lies behind the subjective experience of "not having an equal opportunity to participate," also known as exclusion. We would hazard a guess that you were not expecting to see a heading on "physical pain" in a facilitation book. We hope that by the end of this section you'll think differently about those moments in which someone's contribution is accidentally (or intentionally) ignored.

Have you ever stepped on a LEGO block? The pain that races through your body increases blood flow to a region of your brain called the anterior singular cortex. It also results in less blood flow to your prefrontal cortex (the part of your brain responsible for more complex cognitive functioning). Simply put, you're less likely to do high-quality, complex thinking when experiencing acute pain.

So, what happens in the brain when we experience social pain? In a study, beautifully titled "Broken Hearts and Broken Bones: A Neural Perspective on the Similarities Between Social and Physical Pain," Eisenberger[9] looked at which areas of the brain are activated when someone feels excluded. This study found that the same pathways in the brain activate when a person experiences social pain and physical pain: the dorsal part of the anterior singular cortex. This is interesting when we consider that feelings of exclusion, isolation, and rejection are all forms of "social pain." As mentioned above, in meetings in which certain voices dominate and others are accidentally/intentionally silenced, motivation and quality thinking are compromised. A further cost we pay in such spaces is that some people may perceive the experience as painful, and under such circumstances our brains are activated in a way that is not optimal for complex reasoning.

TYPES OF REMOTE MEETINGS

To consider how we, as facilitators, can make sure that every meeting attendee is able to experience the meeting in a 4×4 we need to start with an awareness of the kind of remote meeting we are holding. Creating equal opportunity to participate and contribute in a remote setting looks different depending on the type of meeting. Typically, there are three generic types of remote meetings (independent of the content of the meeting):

1. **Solo remoting:** A few individuals dial in remotely and the majority of the meeting attendees are co-located in one meeting room, using one screen/audio/video to connect with the remote attendees.

2. **Hybrid:** A few groups of co-located people are dialing in to one call.

3. **Fully remote:** Each person is on the call using their own machine, audio, and video.

Each of these spaces poses a unique challenge in creating equal opportunity.

Consider the first scenario in which one person is on a screen and the remainder of the group is in the room, writing on the board and having a conversation. The individual dialing in does not have the same experience as the rest of the group. Both audio and visual quality compromise their interaction. At worst the remote person is forgotten by the group, at best they attempt to contribute while having a different experience.

METHODS AND MECHANICS

Go Fully Remote When You Can

One way to address the imbalances of power on a remote call is by encouraging everyone to go fully remote; each person dials in to the call on their own machine. Going fully remote in many ways levels the playing field. While there are no perfect solutions to creating equal opportunity, it is the role of the facilitator to creatively seek solutions. We prefer to have everyone dial in remotely regardless of how many people are co-located.

"Otherwise everyone else has an in-person experience with facial expressions and body-language cues except for those dialing in. It's almost as if you are having a conversation in another language."

—Sam Laing[10]

This approach takes a shared commitment to equalizing participation in the group and we recommend that you take this step with buy-in, commitment, and agreement from the whole group. It may help to ask for feedback from all participants on how they experienced going fully remote versus when only some are remote. We acknowledge that for some organizations this may seem like a stretch but we have experienced the value this shift brings to both engagement and meeting outcomes.

A "PSEUDO BODY" AS A SUBSTITUTE

When considering how to create equal opportunity in a meeting, it is important to remain cognizant of the context and purpose of the session. As mentioned above, if someone is remote, our preference is usually for fully remote sessions. However, sometimes other factors necessitate an in-person meeting. Sometimes all but one attendee is co-located and given the nature of the problem, the value of a face-to-face conversation is greater than the need to get the same degree of contribution from the remote person. Often these scenarios pertain to very high-stakes situations. In these scenarios, we think about how to address as many of the variables that make it challenging for the remote person as possible, while simultaneously acknowledging the truth of the trade-offs: the remote person will be unable to participate to the same degree.

An approach we have used a few times for scenarios similar to the above is using an in-person substitute, which we call a "pseudo body." We would like to emphasize that this is a relatively expensive approach and one we only employ when the meeting nature is sufficiently complex and the cost of not harnessing the remote attendee's contribution a genuine concern to the meeting stakeholders. A "pseudo body"

is a neutral, outside person who would not usually be in the meeting, nor has any stake in the outcome. Their role is 100 percent dedicated to relaying information to and from the remote person. This is done by typing context and conversations out to the person, and by walking around the room with the camera if the physical space is being used (possibly showing flip charts or other tangible artifacts). The "pseudo body" also serves as a physical reminder to the group that someone else is present. We have even seen a photo of the remote person stuck on the front of the "pseudo body," with both humorous and somewhat profoundly mindset-shifting results.

Another option to cater to remote attendees is to nominate someone within the meeting to pay specific attention to creating equal opportunity. This might involve transcribing things that are written on posters, checking that the group pauses if someone remote is trying to speak, or assisting when remote attendees have questions. This is a lighter version of the pseudo body that still serves to increase the opportunity for those who are not physically present to contribute.

CHECK TECHNOLOGY IN THE BEGINNING

How you kick off your remote meeting can determine the success of the rest of the session. There are some basic things to keep in mind at the start of your meeting. Once participants start joining the call, you can check whether they can hear you. If you are intending to share your screen, ask if they are able to see the correct screen. Just before you start the meeting and the majority of participants are online you can do one more audio and visual check by asking if anyone is having any trouble. Ensuring that everyone can hear and see adequately is one simple way of ensuring everyone is able to contribute right from the start.

SET UP VIRTUAL STICKIES

A practical limitation of a remote meeting is the unintended technical hiccups and the impact they have on everyone's ability to contribute equally. Consider the likely scenario that someone experiences technical issues and cannot hear. How might their contribution be harnessed? For this reason, we like to have supplementary tools which serve as virtual whiteboards. If someone is struggling to hear or drops off the call, they are usually still able to type and contribute in real time and return to the conversation once their technical issues pass. This also serves to avoid biases toward verbal communication, providing an alternative means of communication for different thinkers.

You may be wondering why we advise virtual stickies (see figures 3 and 4) over video-conferencing chats or in-document line editing. While this kind of writing partially enables contribution, it is insufficient to enable high-quality collaboration. Text typed in a linear sequence (such as a chat tool) cannot easily be edited, combined with other ideas, grouped, and expanded on. These kinds of actions are vital to remote collaboration—we want to give people the option to build on and combine ideas. Thus, we prefer some kind of shape that can contain text and easily be dragged around to build on surrounding ideas and co-create a more complex view of the discussion than was previously available.

FIGURE 3: VIRTUAL STICKIES

What are all the aspects of this issue that we need to consider (Concerns, Benefits, General)?

30 mins

1. Silent writing for 5 minutes (grab a color sticky)
2. Group discussion (25 minutes)

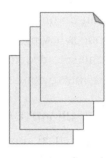

What are all the aspects of this issue that we need to consider (Concerns, Benefits, General)?

30 mins

1. Silent writing for 5 minutes (grab a color sticky)
2. Group discussion (25 minutes)

A few of us will be on leave over the next couple of days. What will the impact be?

I am concerned that the current proposal will take too long (BM)

I am concerned that we don't have all the facts (EB)

Our team should be able to handle this complexity (BM)

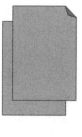

It looks like our current sprint will end early so we should have time to investigate options (EB)

37

How it works (see figure 3):

- Rectangular shapes that look like physical stickies are created prior to the meeting (and copied/pasted to form a stack). Participants recognize the shapes as stickies and have an existing mental model for how to engage with them, despite their being digital

- Participants can grab a virtual sticky and have five minutes to think through the problem

- As we begin discussing what has been written, themes might emerge, and we can group ideas easily by dragging them together (see figure 4)

By allowing people time to write, you allow people time to think, which further benefits groups with different comfort levels with the language being spoken. Reading is available to assist in comprehension, lessening the pressure on verbal communication.

LIGHTWEIGHT MECHANISMS TO DISPLAY GROUP OPINION

Where virtual sticky notes allow us the space to convey and organize information, groups also need mechanisms for enabling decision-making. One such mechanism is dot voting (see figure 5). When faced with a few options for next steps, each participant is given a few dots and asked to place them on the options they prefer (see figure 6). This helps provide visibility on where opinions of the group are trending in a light, nonthreatening way. From here the facilitator has insightful data to inform next steps: maybe there is high agreement and no further discussion is required; maybe opinions vary greatly and it is evident that more time is required to understand the issue.

Instructions

1. Generate ideas for 5 minutes (grab a sticky)
2. Group discussion for 15 minutes
3. Vote and decide with dots for 5 minutes (each person gets 3 votes)

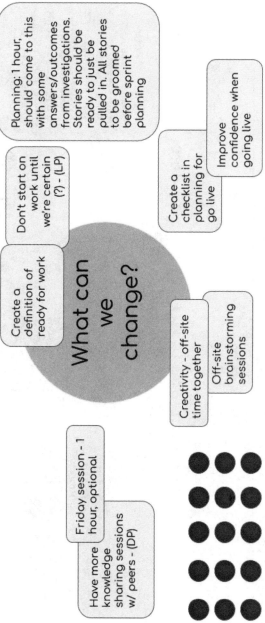

FIGURE 6: DOT VOTING TO MAKE DECISIONS

Instructions
1. Generate ideas for 5 minutes (grab a sticky)
2. Group discussion for 15 minutes
3. Vote and decide with dots for 5 minutes (each person gets 3 votes)

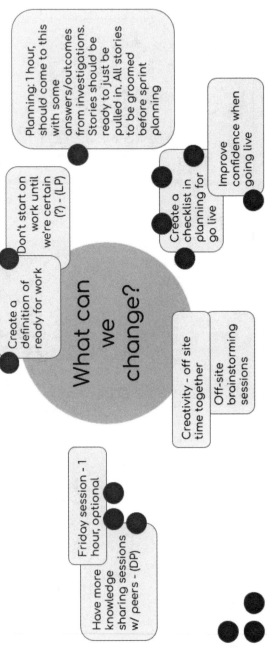

How it works (see figure 5):

- Participants are given a certain number of dots each (bottom left), in this case three

- Once they have an idea of what the voting options are, they will place the three dots on or around their choices

- Once the dots have moved, we can check with the group if everyone has had a chance and then discuss what we are seeing together (see figure 6)

ALLOW TIME FOR PRE-READING

When thinking about how to achieve a 4×4 safari meeting experience, sometimes we like to give people a few minutes in the session to read any relevant content (see figure 6). People may have read this before coming into the session, but often we do not get time to in our busy days or we read it a few days ago and have a patchy recollection of it. If we can spend a few minutes bringing everyone closer in their baseline understanding, the conversation is more likely to be of a higher quality and people are likely to be able to contribute more as the information is fresh in their minds.

How it works (see figure 7):

- The facilitator has allocated five minutes pre-reading time at the beginning of the session

- The question boxes allow people to capture their thoughts and give their perspectives. This may also spark ideas for other attendees

PRE-POPULATE NAMES

There are subtle ways in which a facilitator can draw out participation in a remote space. By simply pre-populating

Reading material
(if you come across anything else, please paste it here)

1. Link 1
2. Link 2
3. Link 3
4. Link 4
5.
6.

PURPOSE

Explore the theory around estimating projects and consider our team's approach

Agenda:
1. Reading [5 mins]
2. Explore main points [25 mins]
3. Consolidate & close [15 mins]

Any questions/ comments

Any questions/ comments

Any questions/ comments

everyone's names on a slide (see figures 8 and 9), the invitation for all attendees to participate is established, and the barrier to contribute is low. This serves an additional purpose of bringing awareness to the humans behind the screens. Sometimes this is easier when videos are on, but often this is not possible and it's all too easy to forget all the humans on a call or to default to paying attention only to those who are the most vocal. By seeing everyone's name, the group is reminded of each person. A secondary benefit is that it can alleviate some anxiety from participants around determining who speaks next and whether everyone has contributed yet.

How it works (see figure 8):

■ Everyone's names have been pre-populated by the facilitator

■ Meeting attendees are invited to find their name and color it based on how they feel

■ Ease of contribution: Coloring a block feels much less threatening than saying "I fear that we won't make it." From here, the facilitator has some helpful data to explore with the group (see figure 9)

PAY ATTENTION TO THE SPACE

Just as we spoke about opening the space by checking that everyone can hear, be heard, and see, this ability to contribute needs to be sustained throughout. Often someone might be struggling to hear but for fear of disrupting the meeting they keep quiet. In so doing, the meeting loses a voice and a perspective, and the outcome's reach might be influenced. As the facilitator, if you can observe the space and notice possible signs that people are struggling, you can use

Go live - 1 month from today

Color your circle based on how confident you feel right now:

- **Green = Super confident**

- Yellow = Slightly unsure

- Red = No way

Ruan

Terri

Jen

Kyla

Thuso

Lee

Go live – 1 month from today

Color your circle based on how confident you feel right now:

- **Green = Super confident**
- Yellow = Slightly unsure
- Red = No way

this information to pause to bring them back. Simply pausing to check that everyone can still hear or sending a message to someone who looks confused can increase contribution.

CHAPTER SUMMARY: CREATE EQUAL OPPORTUNITY

How likely is it that some attendees are experiencing your meeting on a rusty bicycle, while the rest of the group is game spotting from the vantage of a 4×4? The cost of such experiences is paid not only at an individual level, but at an organizational level too. In subtle ways, the facilitator is able to drastically shift the outcome of the meeting, simply by bringing awareness to how interactions in a remote space might affect the quality of outcomes. If people have been invited to solve a problem, it is important that they are both able and trusted to do so. How much time, money, and effort are wasted in meetings where only a few voices are heard? The pursuit of creating equal opportunities to participate is not optional, but vital to the success of our teams and organizations.

Take some time to consider one or two of the questions below in relation to a meeting you are responsible for:

- ❑ **Type of meeting:** How can you get as close to everyone having the same experience as possible?

- ❑ **Technical issues:** How can you prepare for potential technical challenges that may occur?

- ❑ **Language:** What language is being spoken and who might this language choice disadvantage?

- ❑ **Thinking styles:** How can you cater to different thinking styles, such as those who need to speak to think versus those who need time to think?

METHODS AND MECHANICS SUMMARY

1. Go fully remote when you can
2. A "pseudo body" as a substitute
3. Check technology in the beginning
4. Set up virtual stickies
5. Lightweight mechanisms to display opinion (e.g., dot voting)
6. Allow time for pre-reading
7. Pre-populate names
8. Pay attention to the space

PRINCIPLES:

1. Create Equal Opportunity
2.
3.
4.
5.
6.

PRINCIPLE 2: ENABLE FLOW

"You will never reach your destination if you stop and throw stones at every dog that barks."

—Winston Churchill[11]

Cape Town is an incredible city. It is surrounded by the ocean and majestic mountains and has a vibrant city life. Yet, like most major cities, Cape Town has a real traffic problem. When all you want is to get to work to start your day, this start is frequently delayed by a few hours. Similarly, when you want to get home to unwind, a small fender bender can result in an unavoidable gridlock across the city.

No matter how beautiful one's surroundings are, when arriving at one's destination is delayed by frequent, unexpected stops, it's normal to feel tired or frustrated. "Traffic jam" effects can be observed in meetings too. Regardless of how much we enjoy the company, the space, or the content in a meeting, unexpected detours that delay reaching the outcome can lead to tension and fatigue.

Remote meetings are often punctuated with stops and detours that can be avoided with a little planning or guidance. In the absence of behavioral cues, attendees will sometimes interrupt one another, which can make progress feel jerky. The group could be struggling to think together because they are feeling tired, and noticing this is tricky in a remote space. As these little moments of frustration compound, the feeling of being stuck in traffic becomes relatable.

UNDER THE HOOD
WHY "AHA" FEELS GOOD

Our brains are wired to enjoy answering questions and closing feedback loops. When we're seeking an answer or solving a problem a loop is opened. As we reach insight the loop closes and this closure feels good: the positive dopamine kick our brains get propels us forward and onto the next task. Finding that answer to a crossword puzzle feels great and makes you want to keep going.

A research paper by Tik and others, "Neural correlates of the Aha!-moment," found that reward networks are activated in the brain around the moment of insight.[12] This means that when participants experienced relief in having solved a problem, the brain was experiencing more dopamine in regions related to reward: their brains were saying, "This feels good, let's get more."

Let's consider an example at work. If you're trying to remember a decision your team took last week and finally it comes to you, that little zip of energy you feel as the loop closes propels you forward to the next task. The reverse is equally true. When we are inhibited from closing a loop, a few things can happen:

- **We disengage:** We distract ourselves (suddenly Twitter is really appealing)
- **We feel tired:** As we seek closure on another task, the background task is still running and consuming brain RAM
- **We feel frustrated:** We bash our heads against the issue with no success

The flow and resolution of conversations and thinking in a meeting matters. Changes in direction and new information naturally mean that meetings meander and wind down unexpected paths. This diversity of thinking is important in reaching quality outcomes. A facilitator's skill in judging and working with both helpful and unhelpful detours can have a meaningful impact on the outcome.

A skilled facilitator is able to shift and influence the flow of traffic to help the group arrive at their destination. This might mean that if a particular attendee insists on raising a point that the group feels is not relevant to the topic at hand, to maintain the flow of the meeting, action needs to be taken. You might choose to set a time limit (often referred to as a timebox) to the conversation, take an action for a follow-up conversation, or reflect back to the group what you're seeing so that they might choose which path to pursue. For example, "It feels like this point is important, it also feels different to what we're talking about right now. What if we park it here and come back to it towards the end?" This conscious attention to the flow of conversation enables a facilitator to channel traffic.

Channeling traffic is a skill which we believe is especially valuable in remote meetings. The remote environment is particularly vulnerable to disruption and derailment. In the chapter on challenges we spoke about how technical barriers can break flow. As someone drops in and out of a call, all parties are interrupted, and that person struggles to contribute. If the group is trying to close out a point and has to keep retracing their steps to bring someone up to speed, the loop stays open and all parties run the risk of tiring or disengaging. Knowing such challenges exist, how might a facilitator overcome them?

METHODS AND MECHANICS

Manage Expectations: Make the Agenda and Session Rules Visible

We started this chapter with a discussion of traffic. If you know ahead of time where you might get blocked and what to expect, it's much easier to tolerate the delays. Creating clear expectations and rules of engagement (see figure 10) in a session can contribute to the flow of a session purely by preparing people mentally for what is to come. If people know what to expect and what is expected of them, it is easier to contribute. There is no such thing as perfect remote meeting agreements; what matters most is that the group establishes their own norms.

How it works (see figure 10):

- The agenda gives people a sense of what to expect

- Timeboxes further serve the purpose of setting expectations and providing initial guidelines

- The three blocks at the bottom assist people in navigating the space. The group has the option to change or add

FIGURE 10: MAKING THE AGENDA AND SESSION AGREEMENTS VISIBLE

AGENDA

What **principles** are important?

[15 mins]

What **complicates** remote meetings?

[20 mins]

Quick body break

How might we improve the quality of remote meetings?

[25 mins]

Sharing and **close**

[10 mins]

Raise hand to speak

Mute if in a noisy area

It's ok to feel tired. If so paste a

■ The "energy gauge" (yawning emoji) can be used by the facilitator to determine when the group needs to pull over for a quick break

CO-CREATE VISUAL DOCUMENTATION

Working off a shared visual map (see figure 11) of the conversation means that if someone drops off the video or audio, they are still able to follow the conversation (real-time documentation tools are usually less susceptible to bandwidth issues). When the person is able to dial back in, the group will have to repeat less for them as they will have maintained some context and thus will join back in with less disruption to the flow of the session.

If you are working with a group that speaks different languages at home, another common cause for disruption is misunderstandings or the need to repeat information. It is important to go at a pace suitable for everyone. Having a visual replica of the conversation allows attendees the time to read and reread the conversation as many times as needed. This also reduces the likelihood of participants disengaging because they have more time to think and process.

How it works (see figure 11):

■ The group has shapes at their disposal to visualize the conversation as they go

■ The facilitator has pre-created some shapes and can create others as the conversation continues

■ Anyone talking can drag/edit/copy/change something to illustrate their point

■ Slowly a visual map grows as the conversation flows (see figure 12)

FIGURE 11: CREATING ARTIFACTS FOR PARTICIPANTS TO CO-CREATE DOCUMENTATION

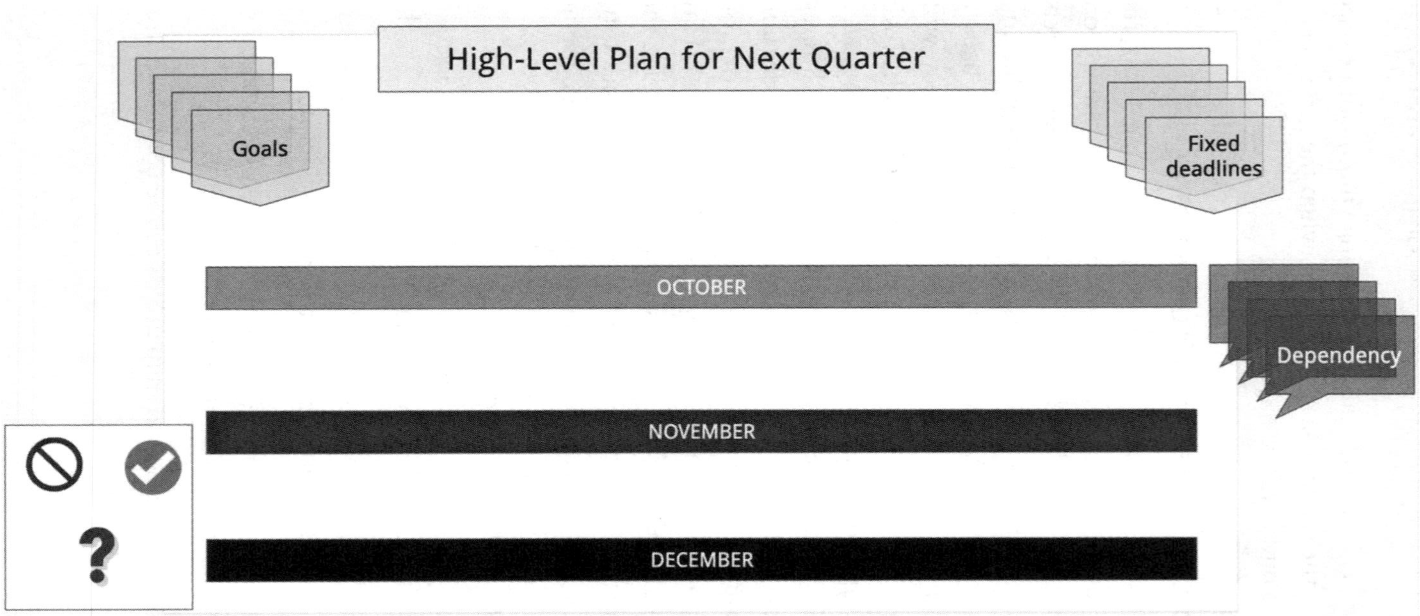

FIGURE 12: PARTICIPANTS HAVE USED THE PREMADE ARTIFACTS

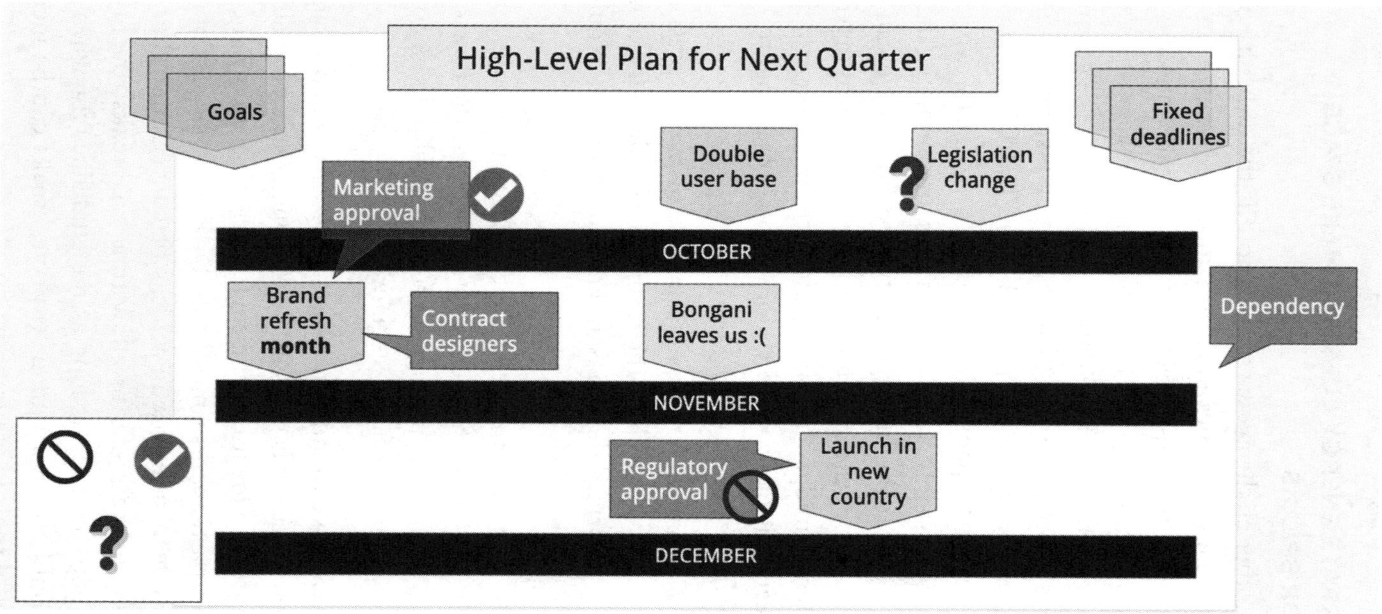

High-Level Plan for Next Quarter

Goals

Marketing approval

Double user base

Fixed deadlines

Legislation change

Brand refresh **month**

Contract designers

Bongani leaves us :(

Regulatory approval

Launch in new country

Dependency

OCTOBER

NOVEMBER

DECEMBER

CREATE ENERGY CUES AND MAKE SPACE
FOR BREAKS

Another challenge we spoke about is the difficulty of reading behavioral cues in remote meetings. These cues enable the team to adjust their behavior (if someone leans in, the group's attention might subtly shift to them to listen) and the facilitator to have data to decide what the group might need in order to reach their destination (as people start looking tired, a facilitator might decide a break is in order). Providing participants with a mechanism to easily express their needs (possibly a change of pace or direction) in a light, easy way can really help the meeting to flow. If we can enable people to feel more in control of the space by having options to nudge the pace and direction of conversation the meeting is likely to flow more smoothly (see figure 13).

How it works (see figure 13):

- By giving participants a mechanism to express how they are feeling, the facilitator is able to make more informed decisions about how and when to guide traffic

- If more than one of the clocks start to move toward the block, the facilitator can see that the flow of the meeting is turning and something should be done to return the flow (see figure 14)

We have found that maintaining energy and focus in remote meetings is particularly challenging and providing brief pauses is a great mechanism for renewing energy. It can also give participants time to step back from the session, which may help stimulate new ideas or conversation. For longer sessions we prefer to allow time for breaks roughly every 45–60 minutes. As long as the guidelines for when people should return are made explicit, breaks can be incredibly useful tools in maintaining flow.

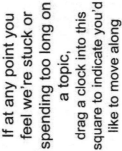

Team Meeting

If at any point you feel we're stuck or spending too long on a topic,

drag a clock into this square to indicate you'd like to move along

We might not move along straight away, but as soon as we see lots of clocks we know something...

Timebox: 2 hours

Topic

Topic

Topic

ROOT PARTICIPANTS IN THE PRESENT

As previously mentioned, one of the tools we like to use is Google Slides. A helpful feature to draw attention to is the summary slide view on the left side of the screen (see figure 15), which looks similar to Microsoft's PowerPoint. Why is this feature interesting? Distractions happen even with the best intentions to focus. When facilitating remotely, giving explicit direction such as, "We are now on slide number 5" or, "If you have any questions add them on slide number 10," can really help the flow of your meetings. It not only allows people to know where to find things but also lets them know where in the meeting they are. You are helping the group think together by focusing the collective attention.

CHAPTER SUMMARY: ENABLE FLOW

Distractions and disruptions are common in remote calls. The greater the disruption, the lower the likelihood of reaching the meeting's destination. When we are stuck in traffic or unable to reach an answer, we often experience frustration, fatigue, and disengagement, all of which work against achieving the best possible outcomes in a meeting. Conversely, when we reach an insight, we feel really good and our brains generate a little "energy," which makes us want to go on to the next task. A facilitator has the ability to guide traffic in such a way that unnecessary jams are avoided and the group is able to flow toward their goal.

Take some time to consider one or two of the questions below in relation to a meeting you are responsible for:

❑ **Distractions:** What are some of the causes of distraction in recent meetings you have attended?

❑ **Flow:** What can you do to improve the flow of conversation?

FIGURE 15: GIVING PARTICIPANTS AN INDICATION OF WHERE THEY ARE

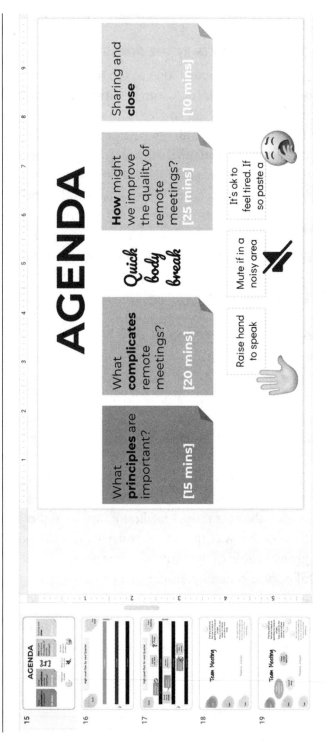

❏ **Energy:** How are you gauging the energy of the room?

❏ **Expectations:** How are attendees' expectations being managed through the session?

METHODS AND MECHANICS SUMMARY

1. Manage expectations: make the agenda visible
2. Manage expectations: make session rules visible
3. Co-create visual documentation
4. Create energy queues
5. Make space for breaks
6. Root participants in the present

PRINCIPLES:

1. Create Equal Opportunity
2. **Enable Flow**
3.
4.
5.
6.

PRINCIPLE 3:
GUIDE WITH VISUALS

*"As bad as we are at remembering names and phone
numbers and word-for-word instructions from our
colleagues, we have really exceptional visual and spatial
memories."*

—Joshua Foer[13]

In the previous chapter we spoke about traffic, its impact
on meetings, and the role of the facilitator in both navigating and guiding it. Another mechanism useful in managing traffic is road signs. Have you ever traveled on a newly
laid road when the lines are still to be painted? It can feel
pretty daunting and confusing. Are you in the middle of the
lane or possibly edging into the lane next to you? Do both
lanes turn left or only one? From painted lines on the road
to physical boards with arrows, visual cues are a critical ingredient in enabling drivers to self-organize on the road.

Every minute on the road, drivers are making numerous
decisions, some conscious and some unconscious. The qual-

ity of decisions we make is related to the information we use when making them. Road signs enable drivers to make nuanced decisions specific to the situation at hand. While each road may be different, signs provide a universal language that enables us to navigate these spaces. Another benefit of road signs is the way they assist in remembering information. It would be impossible to remember our route, what is required of us at each step, and the various requirements of each route. Do two lanes turn right on that highway or one? Is it safe to pass at this part of the road or not? These pieces of information are important for decision-making while driving.

So what relevance do road signs have to remote meetings? A lot is happening in a meeting. We're trying to remember what someone is saying, what was said before, how it connects, and what we'd like to say. We're possibly also trying to remember what was discussed in the past that is relevant to this conversation. To be able to effectively converse and make decisions in a meeting, we need to be able to navigate the space with ease. We need to be able to hold the relevant pieces of the conversation in our awareness in order to compare, analyze, or evaluate them.

Cowan, a renowned researcher in this area, says, "Working memory storage capacity is important because cognitive tasks can be completed only with sufficient ability to hold information as it is processed."[14] In meetings, a group is constantly navigating through tons of information, comparing, analyzing, evaluating, deciding—all cognitive functions which require the brain to hold the concepts under study in mind. How can we, as facilitators, create road signs, visual cues, and reminders that reduce the amount of information people have to hold in their minds, so that their focus and attention can be fully directed to solving?

UNDER THE HOOD
WORKING WITH CONSTRAINED RAM

Despite how we may feel, our brains have a finite capacity to hold information in our conscious awareness. If you have ever tried to memorize a long string of numbers, you'll probably understand what we mean. The circuitry involved in parts of the brain responsible for temporarily holding information while we work with it has limited capacity, and so we tend to only be able to hold a few things in our mind at a time. A famous study arrived at the "magical number seven plus or minus two," in relation to how many distinct pieces of information we can hold at one time.[15] Since then, studies have evidenced this number might be lower, with one making a strong argument for it being around four without participants experiencing a degradation in the quality of information.[16] This number varies based on the complexity and duration of the information being held.

Relating this to the context of road signs, apart from their being a sense-making tool, signs are also a means to reduce the amount of information we need to hold in our awareness. Road signs help to reduce cognitive load, serving as visual reminders of key pieces of information we would otherwise have to remember.

METHODS AND MECHANICS

Enrich Information with Visuals

Identifying key pieces of information in the meeting and representing them visually enables attendees to spend their mental energy on solving the problem at hand, without the effort of recalling the content. The group is then able to prioritize what is important: thinking and solving together. Additionally, many times as conversation continues in a meeting, different people remember different things; if we consider the limits of our working memory, it's highly likely that people are remembering different pieces and building slightly different pictures of the topic and solution.

If our goal with meetings is to reach the best possible outcome, finding ways to help the group focus on what is important and have a shared view thereof is essential. In-person meetings often happen in a space with a whiteboard. Without intentionally replacing this mechanism for visualizing information, conversation in remote meetings can be quite difficult to hold.

Something as simple as a blank, real-time collaborative document provides people an opportunity to co-create a shared reference, guiding everyone on the call (see figure 16). As people write down pieces of information, their brains are able to focus on the conversation. If a previous piece of information is forgotten, it's likely that there is a visual reminder somewhere.

One can take this idea of using visuals to guide conversation a lot further. If we think about the limits of the prefrontal cortex (overloading leads to lack of clear and quality thinking), how might we ease the work on this part of the brain to free up capacity? Could color-coding information make connections easier? What role can images play in helping us to remember concepts? How can the layout simplify the complexity of the problem? Too many road signs can also feel confusing and overwhelming, so how can you strike that balance between feeling lost and overwhelmed?

How it works (see figure 16):

- This visual map is relatively simple. The group has the option to jot down key pieces of information as they go

- The purpose and outcomes are there as reminders

REDUCE COGNITIVE LOAD
WITH CLEAR INSTRUCTIONS

If a road sign tells you there's an off-ramp ahead, it's helpful to be able to look ahead and see that off-ramp approaching. Similarly, on a call, it's helpful for people to see what is expected of them. This does not negate the need for verbal instructions, but rather complements them. If someone is unsure and would usually use contextual cues (such as body language) for guidance, there is now an alternative mechanism for them to get this information.

We'd like to briefly talk about a company-wide demo we facilitated for a huge project. Going into it we were really nervous; the potential for chaos was huge. The audience was fully remote and there were over 150 attendees. Thirty of these people were a part of the project and we really wanted them to be acknowledged for their work—so the demo had 30 co-presenters. Talk about the potential for a traffic jam! We did not have time to practice this presentation, we only had a week to prepare, and a group of

FIGURE 16: SIMPLE VISUAL NOTE-TAKING DOCUMENT

Design Session Monday:

Who:

What:

Outcome:

Actions:
-

Tomorrow:
- Vision and alignment. Phil to go through his docs and give background.
- Getting GOG to understand the context.
-

Potential Epics & Stories:
-

Attendees: Wesley, Bronwyn, Toufeeq

Purpose: Next steps for the project kick off

Outcome: A plan for moving the project forward

Things to be decided:
- When to have project kick off
- Epics and what we need/want
- What can we be ready with on Monday

30 to organize. All planning for this meeting was done asynchronously (more on this in the chapter called After the Call). We relied heavily on visual cues (see figure 17) to signal what was expected both of presenters and audience members.

How it works (see figure 17):

- At this point in the meeting, one person from each team on the project (six teams) gave a quick introduction to their team, what they worked on, and what they were demonstrating

- The names and arrows explained who spoke when

- To keep it engaging for attendees, each speaker added a real picture of their team on the slide while they spoke (they had been prepared for this)

- Timeboxes: Each section had clear time constraints. This meant that we did not have to keep reminding presenters when to move on, and if they forgot, they could just look at the slide

VISUALIZE REMOTE SPACE AGREEMENTS

Remote meetings can be quite ambiguous spaces and so we have found having a quick discussion at the beginning of a meeting to clarify space agreements helps clear up uncertainty. Visualizing these agreements serves as a reminder to the group throughout the session (see figure 18). The content of these agreements is less important than creating the space for the group to think about how they'd like the remote meeting to be. The value of these agreements is in the building of shared context with the participants in the space. Usually common themes that arise are mechanisms

FIGURE 17: VISUALIZING SPEAKING ORDER TO GUIDE THE GROUP

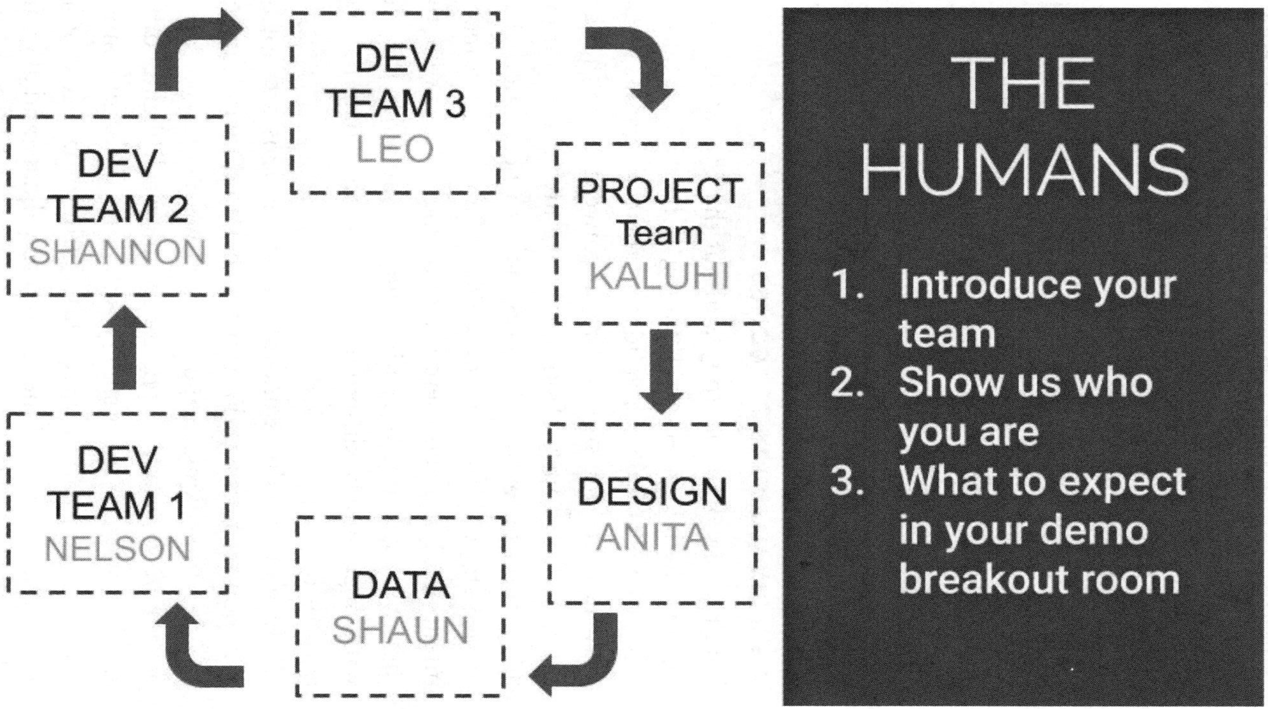

THE
HUMANS

1. Introduce your team
2. Show us who you are
3. What to expect in your demo breakout room

PROJECT
Team KALUHI

DESIGN
ANITA

DEV TEAM 3
LEO

DATA
SHAUN

DEV TEAM 2
SHANNON

DEV TEAM 1
NELSON

to indicate talk turn, muting audio based on noise levels, and clarifying back channels.

How it works (see figure 18):

- We had pre-populated suggestions because we did not have a lot of time

- We had a lot to get through in little time, so instead of interrupting conversation, we established a bell mechanism for marking time

- We asked the group if they wanted to add or change anything and because they felt comfortable we proceeded

VISUALLY VALIDATE OUTCOMES

Finally, we would like to talk about the part of the meeting in which convergent thinking is happening and the role visuals can play in validating the conclusions we are drawing—making sure we are all converging on the same thing, and not just thinking that we are. Have you ever left a meeting with a decision, only to hear another attendee share a different outcome? Why would someone intentionally misrepresent the outcome? It's possible that they were not intentionally doing so, but that they left with a genuinely different understanding of what was agreed to.

Misunderstandings and misinterpretations are not uncommon in meetings. Part of this has to do with the constraints of working memory, which we mentioned earlier: with finite capacity, it's possible we all recall slightly different things. Another possibility is that our different contexts color the information we see differently. Visuals (text or images) can be a helpful mechanism to validate and align understandings (see figure 19).

Getting the best out of today!

Timeboxing
We have limited time so we will timebox sections - listen for the bell

Zoom
If you are battling, please use **chat** to raise issues
MUTE yourself

Flow
Please add **questions** on slide 12

Using the slides
Zoom out so you can see everything
Keep it in **edit** mode

Anything Else....

How it works (see figure 19):

■ In this example, the group had to agree on a plan. We used a visual timeline to take what was in our heads and check our understandings as a group

■ By capturing the action, we had to decide on language choice and in so doing, spotted some misunderstandings that otherwise might not have been made visible

CHAPTER SUMMARY: GUIDE WITH VISUALS

When we think about how drivers self-organize on the road, it's actually pretty impressive. Road signs are a key factor in this organized chaos. Similarly, meetings can benefit from road signs to help people make decisions, recall information, and validate assumptions. As facilitators we can meaningfully improve meeting outcomes if we can visualize information in clear, coherent ways, allowing the finite capacity of the prefrontal cortex to be focused on solving rather than remembering.

Take some time to consider one or two of the questions below in relation to a meeting you are responsible for:

■ **Information:** How many discrete pieces of information are you expecting people to remember in remote meetings?

■ **Perspectives:** How many different views of the discussion at hand are possible?

■ **Instructions:** How clear is it what is expected of attendees at each step of the discussion?

■ **Understanding:** What can you do to validate the group's understanding of the outcomes?

■ **Recall:** What can you do to make it easier for people to remember the concepts discussed?

ACTIONS

From last time	Who	When
Metrics discussion with Devops and our team	Wesley	End of this week
Provide comments to API specs	Technical Work Group	By Thursday
Share documents with the whole working group	Caleb	By tomorrow (July 3rd)

What	Who	When
Share product release documentation	Roxanne	End of today
Discuss deploy to staging for testing	Jacqui	End of this week

UNDER THE HOOD
VISUALS, METAPHORS, AND ABSTRACT THOUGHT

A discussion on the potential of visuals would be incomplete without at least briefly mentioning how visuals and metaphors help our brains to wrestle with and remember abstract concepts. A neuroscientific review of the literature in this field explains that, "Metaphors allow us to draw on concrete, familiar domains to acquire and reason about abstract concepts."[17] This review explores how the easiest concepts to understand are those grounded in sensory experience (i.e., we can physically interact with something). As we move away from sensory experience to abstract thought, it becomes more difficult to comprehend things. This makes sense—the more abstract and distanced reasoning gets from literal experiences, the more challenging it becomes.

The power of metaphor is that it provides a way for our brains to anchor abstract thoughts to something more familiar and comprehensible. In so doing, we are able to better examine and discuss the topic. Have you ever been in a meeting which has become progressively more abstract and as people are struggling to reason about the concepts, someone says something to the effect of, "Let's imagine it like this . . ." and they proceed to create a metaphor for how they understand the concepts. In such situations, the group has been given a thinking tool, a common reference point to ground their thinking. They are far more likely now to have a robust conversation as they are able to hold the concept in mind more easily. Even if they disagree with the metaphor, they are now able to reason about it and build onto it.

The final thing we'd like to highlight regarding the power of metaphor relates to how we remember things. Our brains are much better at remembering things which are connected and grouped into a metaphor than lots of disparate pieces. Joshua Foer spent years studying mental athletes—people who could remember hundreds of binary strings in sequence—and found that metaphor and the linking of ideas played a key role.[18] If people are able to bring to mind what happened in a previous meeting with ease, how much more smoothly will the meeting go? What impact will this enriched information have on the quality of decision-making in the meeting?

METHODS AND MECHANICS SUMMARY

1. Enrich information with visuals
2. Reduce cognitive load with clear instructions
3. Visualize remote space agreements
4. Visually validate outcomes

PRINCIPLES:

1. Create Equal Opportunity
2. Enable Flow
3. **Guide with Visuals**
4.
5.
6.

PRINCIPLE 4:
NURTURE CONNECTION

"Personal connection builds the trust necessary to do the work, and connection to the task unleashes energy."

—Dick Axelrod and Emily Axelrod[19]

Have you ever been delayed on the road by an impossibly slow driver? Maybe the following story feels familiar: You have timed it almost perfectly to arrive at work in time for your first meeting when you get stuck behind an incredibly slow car. It's a single-lane road and you do not get the chance to pass and so you remain stuck, frustration rising every minute. Ten minutes later you're able to overtake, glaring at the oblivious human responsible for this infuriating start to your day. Sound familiar?

Imagine by some magical intervention, the kind that is possible in books when authors are trying to make a point, you are suddenly given knowledge of this driver's story. Having lost his partner in a terrible accident three months ago, the driver, Ric, is battling driving the same route today. While he's finally mustered the courage to start driving again, he is really struggling today. He's using every ounce of courage he can muster.

It's incredible how differently we behave when we understand someone, when we're willing to see the person and their story. If we were driving with the above context, we'd likely be far more tolerant of the driver. In turn, they will not feel the pressure of someone sitting on their bumper or swerving to overtake, and who knows . . . they may even relax a little.

If we are able to connect with someone, we are more forgiving and compassionate and in turn, the other person is more likely to feel safe enough to be themselves. From the SCARF model we learned the importance of relatedness to the brain.[20] As social beings, we perceive the way in which we are being seen and respond accordingly and so our behavior is deeply influenced by the way we are seen by another person. This is beautifully articulated in the book *Leadership and Self-Deception*:

No *matter what we're doing on the outside, people respond primarily to how we're feeling about them on the inside.*

—The Arbinger Institute[21]

It is evident that we are our most authentic self when we are understood by those around us. So if meeting outcomes depend on people being at their peak performance, their most authentic self, how do we create the conditions which foster this kind of connection in remote meetings?

UNDER THE HOOD
THE NEUROSCIENCE OF SOCIAL CONNECTION

We have discussed how our brains are overly sensitive to threat, a helpful survival mechanism but unhelpful in many social situations. We also know that social pain is interpreted in a similar way to physical pain and that this has negative implications for the quality of thinking we can engage in when experiencing social pain. When thinking about social connection, a key aspect is how understood a person feels in any given situation. There is a lot of research that focuses on what happens when we feel understood or misunderstood, and much like social pain, the implications of feeling misunderstood have numerous negative effects.

A study by Morelli and others explored the impact of feeling understood on the brain and resulting behaviors. The study analyzed what happened in the brains of 35 undergraduates when they felt understood or misunderstood. Feeling understood activated reward systems in the brain and neural responses associated with social connection. Whereas, feelings of being misunderstood triggered very similar responses to those identified in earlier studies on pain.[22] In relation to meetings, it is helpful to understand the impact which feeling both understood and misunderstood has on our brain in the moment of an interaction and which condition is more likely to lead to productive behaviors and quality thinking.

Another interesting hypothesis coming from this study is that because people's rewards circuitry is activated, feeling understood may drive individuals to engage in further positive social interactions, as the initial engagement was positively rewarded. If a child says, "thank you" and their mother responds with affirmation, the child is more likely to engage in that behavior in the future. While it may sound like a massive oversimplification, it is worth thinking about what kinds of behaviors our meetings are rewarding. If we think about the kind of behavior that is needed for a meeting to be effective, having people feel self-motivated to engage in collaborative behavior is likely to increase the quality of our meetings. So how do we increase the likelihood that people feel understood in meetings?

Remote work can be particularly challenging when it comes to creating connection and understanding. In-person interactions often accidentally result in connection: we're exposed to tons of data points that can result in connection and in turn, feeling understood. For example, maybe you like someone's shirt and the little compliment you pass makes that person feel slightly more connected to you. We see each other's desks, when we arrive and leave, what online purchases we get delivered to work, and many more things that slowly build connections between people. All of this becomes invisible in a remote space when the only data points one has are those available via a camera.

Creating connection requires intentional effort in remote meetings. There are numerous strategies for doing so, both within a meeting and outside of the meeting space. This chapter will focus specifically on "in-meeting" strategies for both fully remote and hybrid meetings. We will discuss how to foster connection when the call ends in a coming chapter.

METHODS AND MECHANICS

Open the Space with a Check-in Question

At the very start of the meeting, there exists an opportunity to create an initial moment of connection and set the tone for the rest of the time together. If our goal is to help people to see each other as human beings—which, as discussed above, is directly related to our ability to perform at our best—a seemingly innocuous check-in can be a lightweight yet impactful way of improving meeting outcomes.

Depending on what is asked, the question at the start of a meeting can serve multiple purposes. We learned about check-in questions from Esther Derby and Diana Larsen. Something they said has stuck with us:

When someone doesn't speak at the beginning of the retrospective, that person has tacit permission to remain silent for the rest of the session.

—Esther Derby and Diana Larsen[23]

In a remote space it is too easy to remain silent. As Esther and Diana said above, a check-in question can be the first step toward encouraging people to speak. It is also a quick, light way for you, the facilitator, to check if anyone is experiencing technical difficulties in hearing, being heard, or interacting with the tool.

Let's consider a few examples of how these questions might look. Imagine everyone dialing on to the call and the facilitator beginning by saying something to the effect of, "Before we get into the content today, let's take a few minutes to pause and arrive in this space. If you'll humor me, today's check-in question is":

- ■ *"What are you hoping for from today's meeting?"* This brings everyone into the "room," anchoring them in the present, as well as giving people a chance to state their expectations—useful information for the facilitator and group to be aware of. This is also a very nonthreatening, easy question to answer for teams that are not that familiar with one another.

- ■ *"What is something we wouldn't expect to see on your desk?"* or *"Paste an image of yourself doing something you love."* There are lots of light, fun questions that give people the opportunity to share something personal. Although subtle, this can create genuine moments of connection for people on the call, as well as surface things to discuss offline. It also provides a slight reprieve from "seriousness," which we hope goes toward creating a lighter, more effective meeting space. We would, however, like to caution that you use these playful questions with care. Sometimes the conditions surrounding the call (such as high conflict in the team) mean that these questions are inappropriate. Sometimes these questions can be misinterpreted as silly or meaningless, which might have the opposite effect to that intended. We find the more trust we have with the attendee group, the more playful we can be.

■ *"What is your current energy level? Five is bouncing off the walls and one is 'I could climb into bed right now.'"* This question allows for everyone to quickly gauge how everyone else is doing. If we know Shannon is feeling really low, we're far more likely to extend compassion to her throughout the meeting. There is now also an opportunity for someone to reach out to her after the meeting to maintain that connection. If you have a role in this team beyond the meeting, this data also provides the opportunity for you to reach out after the meeting to determine if there are other factors contributing to her low energy. If a few participants are feeling the same, it may be an opportunity for the facilitator to look at the time of the meeting or whether there are other things going on.

WORK IN SMALLER GROUPS

For some, speaking in a large group is intimidating. It is also difficult to create a sense of connection in a big group. Depending on the size of the meeting it may be impractical to hear from every person in the given time. A simple way to lower the perceived barrier to contribution and to harness more opinions in a shorter time is to break into smaller groups and then bring the combined ideas back into the bigger group.

There is something comforting about the sound of murmuring that makes it feel easier to speak up. During in-person meetings, murmur groups—in which people are given a topic to discuss in smaller groups and then relay the summary of their conversation back to the group—break the silence and make it feel easier to speak.

While remote spaces cannot capture the murmuring aspect of murmur groups, they can use the smaller-thinking-groups technique to create a less intimidating environment and increase engagement. Many remote conferencing tools allow you to send attendees into breakout rooms or separate calls. If the instructions for these spaces are sufficiently clear, this is a great way to allow people to connect in smaller groups, have deeper conversations, and be heard.

BE INTENTIONAL ABOUT HOW YOU SHOW UP

We have spoken in previous chapters about the subtle power that facilitators hold. As a facilitator, the group tends to be more influenced by your actions than those of other participants. Here is a chance for you to use your power for good! If you as a facilitator are constantly checking your phone or not being present, you cannot expect something different from attendees. Be what you want to see.

For numerous reasons, remote meetings have a heightened sense of vulnerability. In vulnerable conversations, someone needs to start the circle, to take the first step. If you can be that person on a remote call, your meeting, and over time, your team will be better for it. This will look different for everyone. Maybe you can create light small talk as people are joining the call, taking a genuine interest in how they're doing, their days, or something more personal if appropriate. Maybe taking the first step in being vulnerable will mean sharing how you're feeling, especially if you're struggling a little. If you can share, it will be easier for other people to bring their whole selves to the meeting too.

It's subtle yet powerful. Take a moment to think about how you show up in meetings and what behavior you would like to model. How much of your attention are you giving the meeting?

BRING ATTENTION TO DIFFERING CONTEXTS

It's easy to forget what someone else is experiencing in a meeting. Often once everyone has dialed on to the call, we begin talking about the matter at hand straight away. What if someone is skipping lunch for this call? What if someone has just made dinner for their family and is now skipping dinner for this call? Bringing awareness to differing contexts can go a long way toward fostering connection on a call (see figure 20).

How it works (see figure 20):

- By simply making the different time zones visible in the agenda, participants are reminded of their different contexts

PAY ATTENTION TO THE SPACE

As a facilitator, your role is to make it easy for people to participate. Paying attention to what is happening on the call will provide you with useful data points to help you make in-the-moment decisions about what participants

FIGURE 20: BRINGING AWARENESS TO DIFFERENT TIME ZONES

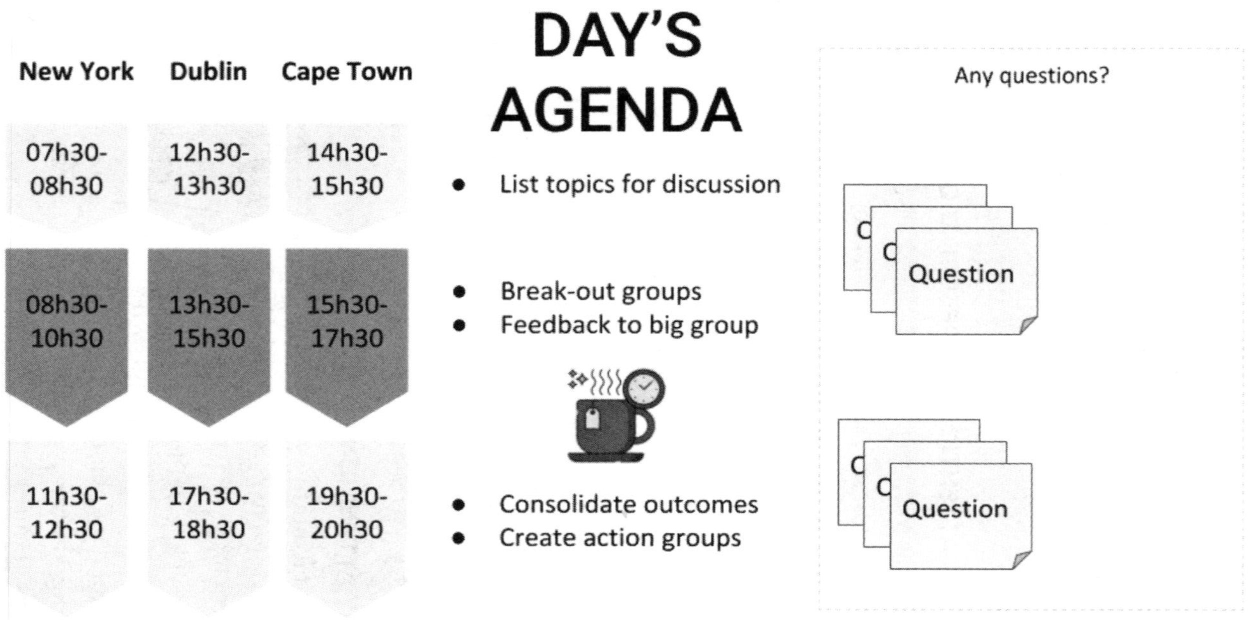

DAY'S
AGENDA

New York	Dublin	Cape Town
07h30-08h30	12h30-13h30	14h30-15h30
08h30-10h30	13h30-15h30	15h30-17h30
11h30-12h30	17h30-18h30	19h30-20h30

- List topics for discussion

- Break-out groups
- Feedback to big group

- Consolidate outcomes
- Create action groups

Any questions?

Question

Question

might need. Oftentimes simply verbalizing what you notice and asking a question can
clarify a participant's experience. For example, "Chen, you
seem to be frowning at your
screen, is everything okay?"

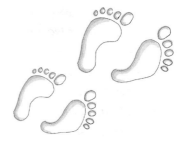

Depending on what tool you are using, participants' actions can hint that they are trying to engage or are having
trouble. You may notice someone constantly muting and un-
muting their mic or they may be looking particularly confused. Either way, simply asking a question will bring the
group's awareness to this person and enable this person to
contribute going forward. You might notice someone speaking but no one can hear them; simply mentioning this can
alleviate some frustration and let participants know that you
care about their experience. For example, "I see, Natasha,
that you're speaking but we can't hear you. Is there a chance
you're on mute?"

MAKE IT OKAY TO LEAVE

It's curious to us how people can feel "trapped" in remote
meetings. A similar phenomenon exists in in-person meetings: people who do not feel that they are giving or getting
value from a meeting remain until the end. Sometimes you
may be facilitating a long meeting where not everyone has to
be present for the entire session. Meetings can be expensive,
and if you know that not everyone has to stick around from
the beginning to the end, make it okay for them to leave.

We love the Open Space rule here known as the Law of
Two Feet or the Law of Mobility.[24] Harrison Owen, the
founder of Open Space, describes it:

*If at any time you find yourself in any situation where
you are neither learning nor contributing—use your
two feet and move to some place more to your liking.
Such a place might be another group, or even outside
into the sunshine. No matter what, don't sit there
feeling miserable. The law, as stated, may sound like
rank hedonism, but even hedonism has its place,
reminding us that unhappy people are unlikely to be
productive people.*[25]

We like to remind people of this in remote meetings. It's
a subtle reminder that behind the little pictures we see of
each other on our screens is a human with needs, and that
it is okay for them to make the decisions that they need to
for themselves. In the case that someone chooses to leave, it
can be helpful to share context via back channels to minimize the risk of negative interpretations and ambiguity.

CHAPTER SUMMARY: NURTURE CONNECTION

How we see people affects the way we show up as well as
the way the other person shows up. It is really important
that your meeting creates the conditions that enable people
to perform at their best. Creating connection on a call is a
key ingredient for holding an effective meeting.

Take some time to consider one or two of the questions
below in relation to a meeting you are responsible for:

❑ **Starting the meeting:** How can you use the start of
the meeting to intentionally set the tone for the rest
of the meeting?

❑ **Facilitator stance:** What example are you providing?

❑ **Attendee context:** What are the different demo-
graphic variables affecting the call you are holding?

❏ **The Law of Mobility:** What might the impact of someone leaving the meeting midway be?

❏ **Meeting space:** What do you notice happening in the meeting that others might not spot?

METHODS AND MECHANICS SUMMARY

1. Open the space with a check-in question
2. Work in smaller groups
3. Be intentional about how you show up
4. Bring attention to differing contexts
5. Pay attention to the space
6. Make it okay to leave

PRINCIPLES:

1. Create Equal Opportunity
2. Enable Flow
3. Guide with Visuals
4. **Nurture Connection**
5.
6.

PRINCIPLE 5:
ENABLE PLAYFUL LEARNING

"Play is our brain's favorite way of learning and maneuvering."

—Diane Ackerman[26]

Have you ever experienced stage fright? Your mind goes completely blank. Try as you may, you cannot bring the information you need to mind. Maybe you get a similar feeling when you are trying to parallel park in front of a café full of people. With so many people watching, a car waiting behind you, and your heart racing, the parking space suddenly seems smaller and you just cannot crack it.

It is comforting to know that you are not alone in these experiences. When our brains detect threat, the chemicals released help us to make quick decisions. To enable this speed, our brain shifts from complex thinking to quick, survival-based decision-making. As frustrating as this response can feel if you are stuck on stage, it makes sense: when we see a lion, we do not have time to contemplate all the possible scenarios that might ensue; we need to make a quick decision.

In today's stressful world, this threat detection mechanism is triggered often. As with the stage fright example, it does not take an actual lion or a parallel parking situation for us to experience stress. It can be the memory of how the last meeting ended that makes your heart race. Perhaps the thought of speaking to a camera feels a little scarier and remembering what you wanted to say becomes a little cloudier.

As you know by now, meetings are innately vulnerable spaces, with lots of uncertainty and often high personal investment in outcomes. If, as facilitators, we do not pay attention to the space we are creating, this vulnerability can easily become fear, and if fear triggers someone's primal response mechanisms, we can say goodbye to quality thinking for that person in our meeting. People sometimes equate playfulness as being unprofessional or inappropriate in a work setting. However, if different mindsets can enable or hinder learning, creating the right conditions in a meeting directly relates to achieving higher-quality participation.

UNDER THE HOOD
WHAT IS HAPPENING WHEN YOU FEEL STRESSED?

We know by now that the prefrontal cortex, the most recently evolved part of the brain, is responsible for our complex reasoning, working memory, and a host of other functions required in meetings. It is also the part of the brain most sensitive to the perception of threat, a.k.a. stress.[27] Stress is subjective in nature and so what one person interprets as being a stressful event may not register for another person (think back to the SCARF model we shared in the chapter on remote meeting challenges). However, what remains universal is the fact that our ability to perform optimally is related to the amount of stress we are experiencing.

When we experience stress, two neurotransmitters start to increase in our brains: noradrenaline and dopamine. Both these chemicals are essential for the functioning of the prefrontal cortex. They put the prefrontal cortex into an "awake" state while also enabling it to perform a lot of its inhibitory functioning, such as blocking out distractions, enabling us to focus.[28]

Neuroscientists have identified an inverted-U relationship between the chemicals noradrenaline and dopamine and cognitive performance: both too little and too much stress impact our performance.[29] Have you ever been on holiday and completely forgotten that you had promised to do something? That's probably because your brain needs a little stress for your prefrontal cortex to operate. Similarly, scientists have found that when exposed to too much stress, cognitive functioning drastically decreases. Studies as far back as World War II show that highly skilled pilots often crashed due to easily avoidable errors. The prefrontal cortex is incredibly sensitive to stress.

Before we return to meetings, there's one last thing we'd like to discuss about "stress chemicals": how long they stay around. While the immediate stressor may disappear (maybe your boss walks away), the chemicals meddling with your prefrontal cortex do not dissipate immediately. General consensus is that it takes somewhere between 10 and 20 minutes for the effects to start wearing off and balance to be restored.[30] This means that even if we are able to acknowledge that there is no longer a threat in our environment, we will not be able to perform optimally for up to 20 minutes. What does this mean for those stressful 30-minute meetings we have?

How can we as facilitators create spaces that give people the best chance of bringing their best selves? How do we enable meaningful, difficult conversations without allowing a flood of fear-based chemicals that would hold some people back? How can we use what we know about fear to give our meetings the best chance of success? What alternatives do we have?

We believe that the mindsets and behaviors associated with play provide powerful alternatives to fear and in turn, meetings. When we are able to trigger playful mindsets, we avoid fear responses by providing our brains with an alternative route to solve problems. According to the LEGO Foundation,[31] playful learning experiences can be characterized by the presence of:

- Joy

- Meaning

- Active engagement

- Iteration

- Social interaction

Don't these sound like wonderful ingredients for a meeting?

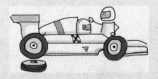

UNDER THE HOOD
WHAT DOES PLAYFUL LEARNING MEAN?

Apart from avoiding the detrimental effects of fear, research makes a strong case for play being a powerful learning mechanism, not just for children but for adults too. According to the LEGO Foundation's review of neuroscientific literature on play,[32] play puts the brain in an optimal state to engage in learning: "Learning in the brain refers to the neural capacity to process and respond to different sensory, or multimodal, inputs, on both basic and complex levels."

In this more open, lighthearted state of play, our brains are far more likely to make new connections and perceive information in a new light. As the complexity of problems that modern organizations face increases, it is crucial that we are able to learn and respond to new problems. To be able to achieve these new insights, we need to get really good at learning—and one powerful mechanism for doing so is to create playful learning experiences.

We want to spend a moment going deeper into the five characteristics of playful learning experiences so that you can look for ways to create these conditions in your own meetings:

- **Joy:** Emotions play an important role in learning; joy in particular is related to increased dopamine, which, as discussed earlier, is related to our reward circuitry.

■ **Meaning:** Our brains use tons of existing mental maps. Meaningful experiences are created when we are able to connect new stimuli to existing data. A little like the satisfaction we get from answering questions and closing feedback loops, for a playful learning experience to be meaningful we need to be connecting and integrating new pieces of information into existing ones.

■ **Active engagement:** The degree to which we feel involved and autonomous when in a situation affects our ability to learn. Active engagement is that sweet spot of feeling involved, empowered, and able to block out distractions.

■ **Iteration:** Iteration is about moving away from perfection and embracing different perspectives. Research has shown that this kind of thinking is more likely to lead to creativity, flexibility, and inclusive behaviors, as people acknowledge that ideas compound and build on one another, rather than seeking absolutes.[33]

■ **Social interaction:** We are highly tuned to detect the social states of others; to foster playful learning experiences, we need to create the conditions in which people feel safe to learn and interact with one another in a positive way.

When you think about meetings, how many of the above characteristics are present? If we want to create meaningful, playful learning experiences in our organizations, we can start by thinking about how to nurture some of these things.

When it comes to bringing playful learning into your meetings, we are not suggesting that suddenly meetings go from outcome-focused conversations to games and frivolity. Rather, we are suggesting that where possible you bring aspects of playful learning to your meetings and that you pay attention to the language you use, the behaviors you encourage, and the tone you set as a facilitator. There are lots of small opportunities to lighten the mood, invite curiosity, and avoid fear in every meeting—you just need to learn to spot them.

METHODS AND MECHANICS

Craft Your Container

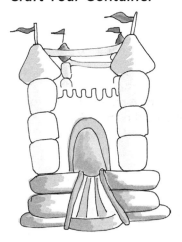

Imagine your meeting as a container. As with the minibus, the taxi is the container and the Gaatjie is responsible for looking after it. You, as the facilitator, are crafting and maintaining the container for the conversation. The way you phrase the purpose begins to craft that container. The way you explain the process further colors the container. How you engage people throughout the session maintains the container.

The container you create will elicit a certain kind of behavior. If you put people in a boxing ring, it is most likely that they will box. If you put people in a bounce castle, it is quite possible that they will play. So what can we, as facilitators, do to create and maintain containers that enable playful learning mindsets?

Consider the difference between these two sentences:

- The purpose of today's meeting is to figure out what happened and to make sure it never happens again.

- The purpose of today's meeting is to explore the factors that led us to where we are. We aim to reach new insights and will hopefully come to some new understandings that will pave a way forward.

If you were in these meetings, how might you respond to the first sentence? It's likely that for many people, threat-alarm bells will start going off in their brains.

We have spoken about how check-in questions can go a long way in creating connections between people on calls. Check-in questions can also begin to spark certain mindsets in meetings. If the question asked has no wrong answer—for example, a picture representing how we see the project at the moment—people are invited to play while still doing some meaningful thinking. Maybe you'll experience a few chuckles and commentary that indicate that people are slowly loosening up. It almost always creates an atmosphere of ease and lowers the barrier to participate.

USE WORDS WISELY

Apart from the check-in question, pay attention to the language you use throughout the session. When asking questions, are you using open or accusatory language? Notice the difference between these two questions:

1. Does anyone see an issue in Kyle's suggestion?

2. What is coming to mind for us as we think about this suggestion?

The first question could easily trigger a stressful response in someone. The second question invites curiosity and exploration, key ingredients in playful learning.

USE FUN AND MEANINGFUL VISUALS

We have spoken about how visuals can play a really important part in signposting remote meetings. Visuals also provide a relatively easy mechanism for bringing in a little lightness and play. Sometimes it is as simple as having a funny image on a slide. We like using gifs, where appropriate, to make people smile and hopefully move everyone one inch away from stress and toward play. If the visual can invite joy while also being meaningful then you are really winning.

The meeting below (see figure 21) was designed to unpack the requirements for a coming audit. Risk and compliance tend to have quite negative connotations for people, due to both the stress and complexity often involved. We used the metaphor of "eating one's vegetables" to make it feel relatable and slightly lighter. If something feels approachable and tangible, we are more easily able to reason about it.

How it works (see figure 21):

- The three phases of the meeting were tied to the guiding metaphor

- Unpacking the requirements: understanding what vegetables to eat

- Planning how to meet the requirements: creating a meal plan

- Actioning that which was agreed: the image of the arrow being used to capture this essence

Risk and Compliance

Purpose: Plan for the coming audit

Understand what vegetables we need to eat

(25 minutes)

Create a meal plan for these vegetables

(25 minutes)

Decide next steps

(10 minutes)

BREAK THE SILENCE WITH MUSIC

Have you ever logged onto a remote call and after you say your hellos an uncomfortable silence grows while you wait for others to join? A technique we like to use (when appropriate) is to join the call early and play some music while waiting for participants to join. We have seen it happen where someone joins the call, hears the music, and instantly they smile. Sometimes you find the back channel chat sparking with activity commenting on the song choice, complaining that it is the Spice Girls, or sharing nostalgia and even asking for the artist's name. By using music before the meeting has even started you are sending a signal that this is not a hostile environment and that people can relax and be themselves.

Another time for use of music is when there is silent writing time for a long period. We have asked participants at the beginning while waiting for others to join to recommend one song each to be played so that everyone has a say in the playlist.

How it works (see figure 22):

- While we waited for people to join we gave the instruction to add songs

- Everyone who was on the call started grabbing stickies and pasting their links

- Instead of checking their phones or emails, this helped bring them into the meeting space and avoid distractions

We'd like to share a story that is both humorous and a lesson in how this can go wrong. We had a new team that was fully remote and so we were putting a lot of energy into making their meetings engaging, meaningful, and fun. Just

While we wait for people to join, paste a link to a song that makes you smile
(there's silent writing coming up…)

before a silent brainstorming activity we asked participants to paste a YouTube link to their favorite song. We did not give any constraints for the kinds of songs we were expecting and we were not paying much attention to the songs we played. Only when we heard the very explicit lyrics of "Boom Boom Boom" by the Outhere Brothers did we realize that the team was thinking about acceptance criteria for user stories (user stories are an approach to capturing project requirements) with this backdrop (to anyone who knows this song, you will understand the moral dilemma that ensued for us). It was an *interesting* exercise in maintaining composure and deciding how to respond in the moment, maintaining respect for the attendees above all. We paused the song and the team's composure gradually cracked—and despite our fears of how this might have been interpreted, it has become one of the team's favorite memories that we still laugh about.

While the above story ended well, we have learned to create slightly more clear constraints for the kinds of songs we play. Consider social connection and respecting cultural difference by being mindful of what music you play. Thinking with lyrical music can be a challenge, and the volume of the music matters too. We do not use this technique often, but once in a while it can be fun.

INVITE A LITTLE JOY

As a facilitator thinking about fear and play, if you are able to bring joy and humor into your meetings in an authentic way, you can subtly shift the tone and influence the outcomes. Maybe something funny happened during the week and there's a way to reference it on a slide. If you're working in a team space, maybe they have some inside jokes that you can bring up. All these little, seemingly insignificant moments of humor slowly tell our brains that we are safe and that there is no threat to respond to, and then all the beautiful connections that arise when we feel at ease can begin to spark. In this way, we invite quality thinking into our meetings.

CHAPTER SUMMARY: ENABLE PLAYFUL LEARNING

Just as modern working environments are increasingly stressful, they are also calling for greater degrees of creativity and complex problem solving. This presents an interesting challenge: the default response that stress elicits inhibits our ability to solve complex problems and be creative. If, as facilitators, we can create meeting spaces that trigger playful learning instead of fear, we are giving the group the best chance of achieving creative and powerful outcomes. Where fear and stress can hold us back in meetings, play can unlock infinite potential.

Take some time to consider one or two of the questions below in relation to a meeting you are responsible for:

❏ **Containers:** What kind of container are you creating for your meeting attendees?

❏ **Visuals:** How can you use visuals to lighten the mood?

❏ **Music:** What might happen if people joined the call to the sound of their favorite songs?

❏ **Joy and humor:** What humorous moments have happened recently among your teams?

METHODS AND MECHANICS SUMMARY

1. Craft your container
2. Use words wisely

3. Use fun and meaningful visuals
4. Break the silence with music
5. Invite a little joy

PRINCIPLES:

1. Create Equal Opportunity
2. Enable Flow
3. Guide with Visuals
4. Nurture Connection
5. **Enable Playful Learning**
6.

PRINCIPLE 6:
MASTER YOUR TOOLS

"A bad workman blames his tools."

—Daphne du Maurier

Think back to our minibus taxi. A minibus is a mechanism to get from one point to another. As passengers jump in, there is implicit faith placed in the driver that they know how to drive their vehicle. The time for learning is not while there are 20 innocent paying passengers sitting behind the driver.

Just as a minibus is a vehicle for transporting a group from A to B, a tool in a remote meeting assists in helping the group to reach their destination. While a really fancy vehicle can make the journey more enjoyable, trying to drive a fancy vehicle without knowing how to drive it will frustrate your passengers and possibly cause harm.

It is often tempting when planning a remote session to want to use exciting tools, hoping that it will add to the energy and flow of your sessions. However, if you are unable to drive this tool, you run the risk of relinquishing control to your tool. Furthermore, if insufficient thought has gone into the purpose and planning of the session, the tool may inadvertently decide this for you. In this chapter we get practical and discuss things to consider about tools so that you are in the driver's seat.

START WITH A PURPOSE

Do not let your love for a tool dictate what you will use. Start with the purpose and the desired outcome for the session; trying to understand the desired outcomes and what kind of thinking will be required to achieve them will help you to choose a tool. Once you have your intended purpose and outcomes, it may be useful to work backward, considering which types of artifacts you might need to achieve those outcomes and then decide which tool might be most appropriate.

We have seen that meetings so often become servants to the tools being used. You are in a meeting and someone has spent a few minutes looking for a way to undo what was just done on screen. Or maybe the tool we are using will not let us paste for some reason, so we all watch (and yawn) while links are manually copied across. Does any of this sound familiar?

When thinking about meetings and tooling we need to think about what we need to optimize for and then choose the tool—not the other way around. It's perfectly fine to use one tool for collaboration in a meeting and another tool for the documentation of outcomes. This feels relatively natural in co-located meetings (we use whiteboards in the session and someone commits to document outcomes after the session). Yes, this means that there may be a little extra work capturing outcomes—but how much lower is this cost than sacrificing quality thinking in the session in order to simplify knowledge management across the organization?

If you need to be creative in a meeting, use a tool that enables creative thinking—probably something that is easy to use, visual, and allows real-time collaboration. Consider what kind of thinking your session requires and choose a tool that enables it, not just the one you'll be using to capture outcomes and tag action owners. If you do not, your meeting outcomes will remain stuck within the confines of your tool.

ARRIVE PREPARED

Remote sessions generally require more preparation than in-person sessions. Once you have established what outcomes you need and how you will run the session, you must also ensure that you put in the work to create whatever artifacts are needed. For example, if you want participants to brainstorm answers to a question and you have established that you need digital sticky notes, then preparing that beforehand will improve the flow of the session by reducing wasted team effort on menial tasks. This way no one's time is wasted watching someone perform an administrative task in the session and everyone can easily focus on the activity at hand.

Another aspect to preparation is ensuring that everyone has easy access to the tool you want to use. Sharing a link beforehand and asking participants to check if they are able to access it saves time in the session. It can also allow for participants to play around and familiarize themselves with the tool if they have not been exposed to it yet. It can be frustrating for both you as a facilitator and the participants to lose 10 minutes of a meeting waiting for people to log in: picture

20 people waiting on a bus while one person spends 10 minutes trying to walk through the door, unsuccessfully.

PIVOT WHEN NECESSARY

Just as in in-person meetings, things seldom go according to plan. As a facilitator, your role is to support the group in achieving their outcomes. This might mean changing direction when something has come to light in the session and spending the rest of the session exploring that direction. Often when we have prepared a well-thought-out remote format we are more hesitant to change direction. Maybe you have a slide you really love coming up. Maybe the technique you had planned was going to be really interesting. Keep your purpose front of mind at all times and be willing to toss your tool in favor of serving the group.

BACK CHANNELS AND PAIR FACILITATION

Another aspect to consider is how you will cater to people struggling on the call in a way that does not hold the entire group back. Back channels, pairing on facilitation, and secondary tool options are backup mechanisms that will help you handle in-the-moment complications. For example, if your intention was to use Zoom for video call, you can state that should Zoom encounter a hiccup, Slack will be used for further communication. Another invaluable option is to have a co-facilitator if possible; we have found when pairing it is easier to have one person deal with the administrative side and technical details while the other is focused on the group as a whole and ensuring the session is moving forward.

SEPARATE MEETING ARTIFACTS FROM OUTCOMES

Let's think about how a traditional whiteboard functions in a co-located space. The whiteboard is a thinking and collaboration tool. A team could use it to brainstorm ideas, creating a messy spider web as they go. This whiteboard visual is not intended to be beautiful or complete, it is a tool to aid thinking. Thus, provided there is a photograph or some mechanism to capture the content that was created, it is unlikely the group will be disappointed when the mind map is erased.

We have observed an interesting tendency in remote meetings: the use of remote collaboration tools often leads to an attachment to meeting artifacts, which drives unhelpful behavior within the session. A team may be using a certain tool to enable them to think visually, together. However, as the artifact being created grows, it can occur that the attendees start neatening and "beautifying" the artifact, for example by deleting unnecessary comments or summarizing points. This desire to have a coherent outcome can begin to shadow the more important work to be done in the session—the actual "thinking together" part. Capturing outcomes is essential. However, this is an activity that should commence once the thinking is concluded. This activity does not require the whole group's time and thus can be done asynchronously. Just as we wipe clean a whiteboard once it has served its purpose, it is okay to throw away digital meeting artifacts.

An example of an artifact can be seen in figure 23.

Notice how it looks slightly messy, there are comments scattered around, and you can clearly see that the team's thought process has been made visible. Rather than trying to make this neat as they progressed, the team focused on the conversation at hand.

Figure 24 shows an example of how a team might capture these outcomes after the session.

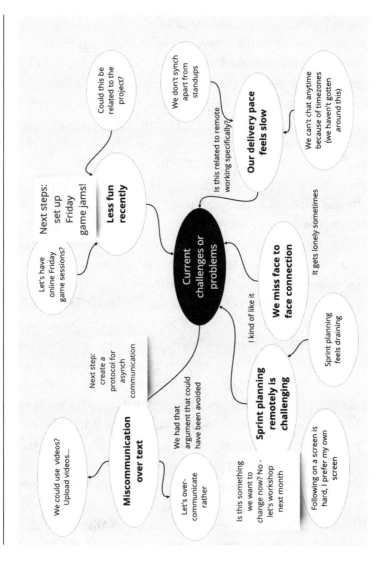

Meeting Summary:

Purpose: Explore current challenges faced with remote working and identify opportunities to improve

Outcomes:
1. Create a protocol for asynchronous communication (Andrea and Monique - 20 Dec)
2. Friday Game Jam sessions (Thabo and Ayesha - 15 Dec)

Open Topics:
- How do we improve sprint planning?
- Delivery pace concerns

Link to meeting notes: www.miro/sdasdd....

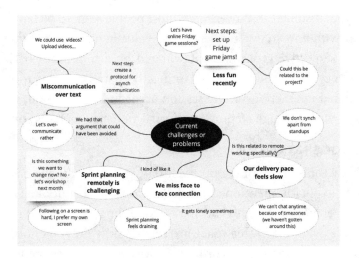

CONSIDER ACCESS AND SECURITY

As facilitators, we have found our personal default has often been to focus on the human nuances of meetings. Security and tool access were not things that came to mind initially for us. However, they are important logistical considerations that can have significant consequences. If you decide to use a free tool, ensure that you are not compromising your company's security. When thinking about user access, we usually prefer tools that do not force attendees to create accounts, as this can be a big deal for some people.

We often default to Google Slides because it is free to use, easily customizable, simple, and safe to share (permissions can be set at various levels). Additionally, because Google Slides is similar to PowerPoint, most people seem to be familiar with how to use it. There is still value in making sure that the respective group being facilitated by a tool has a basic fluency in it and if not, adapting the complexity of tool-related interactions in the session accordingly. That said, we still walk through step-by-step instructions for each session.

CHOOSING A TOOL

New tools are popping up every day, which is why we have not explicitly mentioned particular tools in this book. The movement of remote working is expanding rapidly and the tools available in this space are too. So how do you choose a tool? Apart from access and security, we consider the following:

- **Collaboration tools:** If you are looking for a tool to facilitate collaboration it needs to be intuitive, easy to understand, and flexible. This probably means it has the ability to configure visual elements on the fly and move them around (i.e., group them or connect them) easily. Apart from the features of the tool, the most essential aspect for us is smooth, easy, real-time editing by multiple users.

■ **Conferencing tools:** Tools that are used to meet online ought to be our highest-quality tools. If you are able to spend money, spend it here—poor audio and video can be very distracting. As such, we look for tools that have built-in solutions for bandwidth issues. We also love tools that enable screen sharing, screen annotation, voting/polls, and breakout rooms.

■ **Presentation tools:** If you are presenting a lot, collaboration may not be needed, but keeping people engaged is. When looking for tools to complement presentations we look for ways to have questions visible and possibly ranked based on opinions, the ability to get feedback easily, and a channel to allow parallel text-based discussion among participants.

CHAPTER SUMMARY: MASTER YOUR TOOLS

Just as a driver who is still figuring out how his vehicle works puts their passengers at risk, a facilitator who does not understand their tool puts the whole session at risk. Spend some time before your meeting getting comfortable with your tool. Fit-for-purpose, accessible, and safe tools are far more helpful than fancy ones that you are not quite sure how to drive.

Take some time to consider one or two of the questions below in relation to a meeting you are responsible for:

❏ **Purpose:** What are you trying to achieve with the meeting?

❏ **Preparation:** What can you do before the session that will make the experience smoother for everyone?

❏ **Accessibility and security:** How familiar are you with the security policies of the tools you are using?

METHODS AND MECHANICS SUMMARY

1. Start with a purpose
2. Arrive prepared
3. Pivot when necessary
4. Pair facilitation
5. Back channels
6. Artifacts are not synonymous with outcomes
7. Consider access and security
8. Choosing a tool

If you'd like to know more about which tools we enjoy using and the basics of how to use them, we keep an updated list on our website, available here: https://theremote coaches.com/resources

---

PRINCIPLES:

1. Create Equal Opportunity
2. Enable Flow
3. Guide with Visuals
4. Nurture Connection
5. Enable Playful Learning
6. **Master Your Tool**

AFTER THE CALL:
HOW TO MAINTAIN CONNECTION
WHEN THE CALL ENDS

L et's imagine you are on a remote call and things are wrapping up. Maybe you are busy summarizing actions or asking the group if there is anything still to be said. The conversation has been rich, the engagement high, and you are feeling positive about the impact this meeting will have for the team. Everyone says goodbye and the call ends. The group goes back to their day and there is silence until the next meeting.

Meetings are high-energy moments. Collaboration, thinking, and focus make them unique opportunities for connection in the day. However, these should not be the only moments where collaboration is nurtured in your team or organization. This chapter will focus on what you can do after the call, both immediately as the call ends and with the time in between meetings.

AMPLIFY IMMEDIATELY

The minutes after the call, when the interaction is still fresh in everyone's minds, are really valuable. By reiterating anything that happened (whether it was actions committed to or really human moments of connection) you increase the chance of it being remembered by the group. If little paths were created in our brains, immediately reinforcing them increases the chance that they will remain. As a remote facilitator, you really want to amplify the healthy stuff that happens so that it happens more and more often. Before you know it, these things which you so carefully nurtured will be assimilated into the team's culture.

Some practical examples for how you might amplify immediately:

- Send an email with a screenshot of the outcomes/decisions/actions.

- If your organization uses a messaging app (e.g., Slack, Skype), send a message thanking everyone and sharing a line or two about any observations you had: "Thanks for that everyone. I really enjoyed the energy, it felt like we had a really good conversation."

- Include a unique detail about the meeting in your communications. Maybe someone's child popped into the screen briefly. Remind the group of this connection because in so doing, you are reminding them of the people behind the screens. It can be as simple as adding, "Please send Quinton our love and thank him for making an appearance ☺"

- Send a short line saying goodbye. This simple action creates a small moment of connection after the call, albeit fleeting. Maybe include a reference to the different time zones to acknowledge all the different perspectives: "Bye everyone, I'm going to grab a coffee. I hope you have a good day or evening."

DEAL WITH FALLOUT

Have you ever been on a call where you sensed friction? Maybe a nasty comment was made or someone stopped speaking and you could read the frustration in their expression. It is easy for conflict to be overlooked or ignored in remote spaces. When the call ends, the issue becomes invisible and it requires intentional effort to connect with the relevant people afterward to reach resolution. If these moments of conflict are not addressed, they can fester and create dysfunction that becomes increasingly more difficult to deal with, especially in a distributed environment.

Naturally, this is a sensitive space and requires context-based responses and intuition as to what the specific situation and people require. If something uncomfortable happens on a call, a natural response is to hope that it will be better next time. Avoid the temptation to be hopeful in remote spaces. Be intentional about addressing issues because they seldom resolve themselves. If someone behaved in an offensive manner on a call, find a way to give them constructive feedback afterward. If someone seemed really down, reach out to check that they are okay. The quality of your remote meetings will be impacted by the quality of interactions surrounding these calls.

ASYNCHRONOUS COMMUNICATION

Meetings are a form of synchronous communication, as is texting someone and expecting an immediate response. If we consider that a lot of distributed companies have chosen flexibility and access to skills outside their location over co-location, then we need to be mindful that synchronous communication can be at odds with these goals. Time zone differences and the value placed on flexibility mean that an overreliance on synchronous communication can create rigidity: people have to be online regardless of their time zones and other needs.

An example of asynchronous communication could be someone creating a document with a suggestion, sending it out for comments, and setting a deadline for comments (e.g., three days from now). In their own time, participants can add comments, ask questions, and build on each other's ideas. If there is high consensus and clear outcomes then a meeting is not required. If there are points of contention then a specific meeting for that purpose can be called.

When thinking about introducing more asynchronous ways of communicating and connecting in your team, the following guidelines can be helpful:

- **Trust by default:** If you do not get a response immediately, rather than assuming ill intention, trust that the person is doing what they need to and will reply when they can. Do not expect an immediate response.[34]

- **Over-communicate:** If you are using text, misunderstandings are possible—so if in doubt, over-communicate.

- **Create constraints:** So that making decisions and taking action do not take too long, setting constraints in the document can help. This could mean deadlines for responses or clearly framing next steps if a certain condition is reached (for example, 20-plus comments are unresolved).

We maintain that face-to-face meetings are important for creating connection and solving complex problems. We also acknowledge that sometimes meetings happen that could have been emails. Asynchronous communication is a really valuable tool for teams to maintain productivity and collaboration outside of calls.

REPLICATE IN-PERSON INTERACTIONS

If we consider that meetings are influenced by the quality of the connection between the individuals involved, how might we work on building that connection outside meetings? If we are thinking in the context of co-located office space, there are a lot of coincidental moments that build connections for in-person teams. Maybe it's having some fun together at the PlayStation or chuckling while you hear your colleague cursing at their computer. All these little moments present unplanned opportunities to connect. It's a little more difficult for incidental connection to happen for remote teams. However, that does not mean that it is not possible.

We often start conversations with new distributed teams, bringing awareness by asking something to the effect of, "Given that we're a remote team, we're going to miss out on some of the in-person things that we have all probably enjoyed at some point in our career. What are some of the things you have enjoyed about being on a team?" When people start thinking about these things it provides an opportunity to get creative about how we mimic them in remote spaces. Some things that some of our teams have come with have been:

- **Music:** Creating team Spotify playlists that we keep adding to

- **Watercooler talk:** Having a running call open that anyone can join while working, not with the intention to talk but just to feel like we're working together and to pass the occasional comment

- **Virtual games sessions:** We love the Jackbox games available on Steam. A few teams play these games together once in a while, and they're a bit like virtual board games

There's a lot of room to get creative here and it is important that you allow your team the opportunity to choose. If they suggest or decide to try something, it is more likely that they will be invested in its success. Ask the question and let them find their own answers.

REMOTE TEAM AGREEMENTS

Creating fun mechanics and discovering what a team enjoys are not the only conversations a team needs to have. Another important consideration for teams is agreement on how they will perform other team-related activities in a distributed environment. Making these agreements explicit is fundamental in setting up your distributed space. How your team behaves when they are not on calls will filter into how they behave when on the calls. How will we give feedback? If we cannot see each other speaking, where do we make conversations being had visible? How do we manage expectations of availability? There are lots of questions to choose from. Allow your team to think about how to be a team in a remote space and to establish some baseline agreements.

CHAPTER SUMMARY: MAINTAINING CONNECTION WHEN THE CALL ENDS

When thinking about remote meetings, the time after the meeting can be leveraged to embed the outcomes achieved and nurture a collaborative culture over time. While the meeting is fresh in people's minds, the time immediately after the call can be used to remind people of actions and extend personal connections made. Conversely, if something unhelpful or potentially harmful happened in the meeting, be sure to follow up offline and as far as possible, reach a healthy resolution to set future engagements up for success. Finally, looking beyond traditional meetings, there is an opportunity to find mechanisms for connection with teams that mimic in-person interactions, such as having fun together.

Take some time to consider one or two of the questions below in relation to a meeting you are responsible for:

❑ **Amplify:** What happened in a meeting recently that you would like to see again in a coming meeting?

❑ **Dysfunction:** How have you dealt with tension in remote meetings in the past?

❑ **Fun:** How might you introduce a little fun to your remote team?

TECHNIQUES SUMMARY

1. Amplify immediately
2. Deal with fallout
3. Asynchronous communication
4. Replicate in-person interactions:
   a. Create a playlist
   b. Running meeting for watercooler talk
   c. Virtual game sessions
5. Remote team agreements

TYING IT TOGETHER

The value of having effective and high-quality meetings cannot be overstated for organizations. Our intention with this book is to improve the quality of remote meetings by empowering remote facilitators with actionable methods grounded in principles. Earlier in this book we told three true stories that illustrated some of the common challenges experienced in remote meetings. In this chapter we retell two of these stories to illustrate how you might weave together what you have discovered. Finally, we conclude by grouping what we have discussed into three different perspectives: the principles, the science and the practices.

THE STORY OF A CO-LOCATED TEAM
THAT TRIED REMOTE WORKING

Remember the team that was comfortable in person but struggled in remote meetings? The group norms that they unconsciously relied on had become invisible. The remote meetings accidentally favored verbal communication, which took more effort than expected. The technical barriers they experienced interrupted flow and overall, their meetings felt slow and uncomfortable.

Below is a series of snapshots from one of one of their later Sprint Reviews (see figures 25, 26, and 27). For those not familiar with Agile frameworks, the Sprint Review is a Scrum meeting in which the team comes together at the end of an iteration (a timebox in which they agreed to complete a certain piece of work). The purpose of a Sprint Review[35] is to allow the team and interested stakeholders to look at what has been built, provide feedback (maybe something was not built the way someone had imagined it would be), and then to use the outcomes of this feedback to inform and update the overall plan.

When setting the frame for the session, we brought attention to group norms and allowed the group to add/change the ones we suggested (see figure 25). We did not need to spend much time here. However, this simple upfront acknowledgment provided clarity, which simplified interactions in the session.

Sprint Reviews can feel a little tense. The remote team meetings had a history of tension and so we chose to bring people into the space with a check-in question (see figures 26 and 27) that invited lightness as well as got people thinking creatively about how their last cycle of work went. What was interesting is that some of these metaphors were used to explain things in the rest of the session and came up again in the retrospective. There were smiles, sighs, and nods of agreement as people shared their perspectives. The atmosphere felt lighter and as facilitators we had the sense that people were feeling a little more engaged and connected in the space.

Each slide had some kind of writing mechanism for the attendees who needed time to think, felt hesitant to inter-

Purpose: Evolve our plan by looking at what was built and what that means for next sprint

1. Quick check-in [5 mins]

2. Demo complete stories [20 mins]

3. Adapt the plan [20 mins]

4. Anything to add?

How do you feel about this sprint?
Find a picture to represent it...

5 mins

How do you feel about this sprint?
Find a picture to represent it...

rupt but wanted to raise a point, or were not quite sure how to add what they wanted to. These sticky notes, which we had pre-created and left empty, filled up quickly and decreased the frustration and anxiety that had previously resulted from not being heard. We also discussed some interesting topics as a result of what was written.

As far as possible, we tried to capture the conversation visually to make it easy for the group to think together. We had a screenshot of the team's virtual sprint board (see figure 28) so that people had easy access to information without having to search through tabs and risk getting distracted. Timeboxes and instructions were made visible. At times people struggled with audio, yet they could still see what was being written and did not lose too much context. As such, the impact of technical glitches on the whole group was minimized (see figure 29).

Once we had finished looking at the work we moved the discussion to reflect on the project plan. We worked off an existing timeline that the team was working on (see figure 30). While it is not perfectly neat, the intention was for it to be easy to see and add to the timeline (we had a more accurate one that we would update offline). We allowed time for people to write ideas (which is how the sticky notes came to be filled) and we moved the blocks on the timeline based on the discussion (see figure 31).

Finally, we concluded the session by going through the previous slides and copying anything that looked like an action to this slide (see figure 32). People did this together so it went really quickly. Then we asked the simple questions: "Who will own it?" and "By when will it be done?" and in so doing, we summarized actions from the meeting.

Overall, the meeting flowed more smoothly as a result of the increased clarity and ease of contribution. The small mo-

FIGURE 28: SCREENSHOT OF THE TEAM'S VIRTUAL SPRINT BOARD

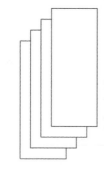

Feedback/Questions

Review what was completed

1. Look at each story that was **completed**
2. Share your screen and demo

Sprint •••   ☆   Personal   🔒 Private   Invite

To Do

Create UI for whitelisting

+ Add another card

In Progress

Disable certain buttons based on user permissions

+ Add another card

Review

Update Terms and Conditions

+ Add another card

Done

Enable a user to logout

Verify credentials

Change colours to conform to new brand standards 🖉

+ Add another

20 mins

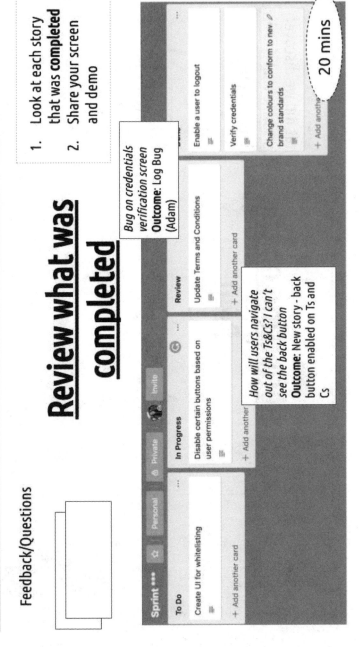

FIGURE 30: VISUALIZING A PLAN USING A TIMELINE

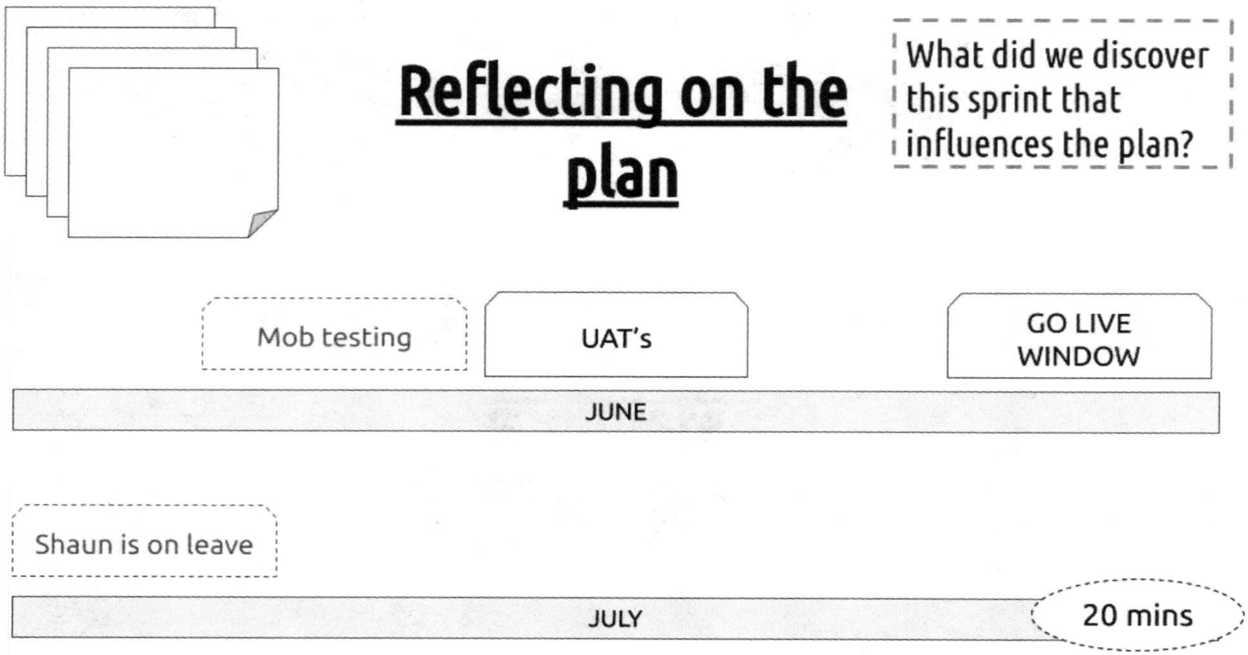

Reflecting on the plan

What did we discover this sprint that influences the plan?

Mob testing

UAT's

GO LIVE WINDOW

JUNE

Shaun is on leave

20 mins

JULY

Reflecting on the plan

What did we discover this sprint that influences the plan?

New stories this sprint might mean that we're a bit delayed.... share outcomes with stakeholders

Design team has requested more changes
Action: offline discussion, no changes yet

Mob testing

UAT's

GO LIVE WINDOW

JUNE

Shaun is on leave

GO LIVE WINDOW

JULY

20 mins

131

FIGURE 32: RECORDING ACTIONS FROM THE SESSION

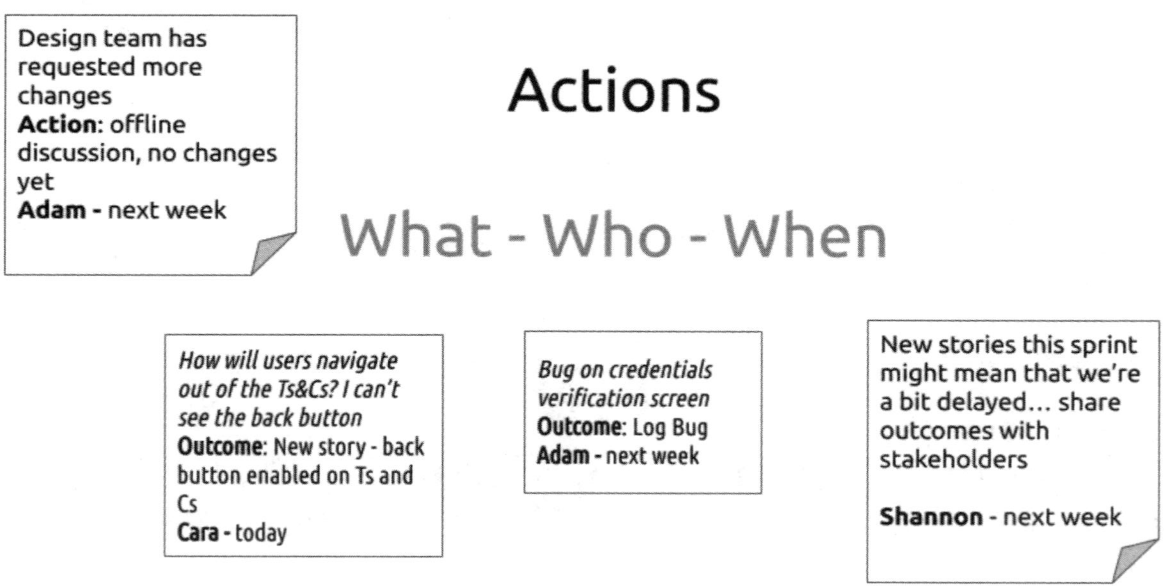

Actions

What - Who - When

Design team has requested more changes
Action: offline discussion, no changes yet
Adam - next week

How will users navigate out of the Ts&Cs? I can't see the back button
Outcome: New story - back button enabled on Ts and Cs
Cara - today

Bug on credentials verification screen
Outcome: Log Bug
Adam - next week

New stories this sprint might mean that we're a bit delayed... share outcomes with stakeholders
Shannon - next week

ments of joy shifted the group toward feeling more positive and engaged. Where they had accidentally been biased toward verbal communication, the group now had written and visual communication available to them too. Pre-prepared mechanics meant that communication in the session felt easier and smoother. The team, once again, felt that their meetings were achieving meaningful outcomes.

THE STORY OF THE FULLY REMOTE PROJECT KICKOFF

Now we'll return to the story of the fully remote project kickoff where there were over 20 people, from three different countries, with very little familiarity. The size and diversity of the group posed interesting challenges. We were mindful that not everyone felt comfortable speaking English. We also knew from discussions prior to this meeting that one of those locations was experiencing provider-related Internet issues and so we suspected that technical difficulties might arise.

A lot of work went into the preparation for this session, some of which involved finding out the purpose and outcome from the project sponsor. Once that was established, we spent 10 minutes beforehand with each of the attendees to understand what their expectations were and what they needed from the session. This was an important step in understanding the different perspectives that would be in the space. There were a few loud voices with strong opinions, so providing spaces for the whole group to have thinking and writing time was a power-distribution mechanism.

Right at the beginning, one of the first concepts we introduced was a "parking lot." We explained that anyone could add a sticky note with a topic of conversation that required further exploration offline (see figure 33). This allowed any-

Parking Lot

If further discussion is needed offline, add your comment on a sticky note here. **Please add your name** so we know who to follow up with.

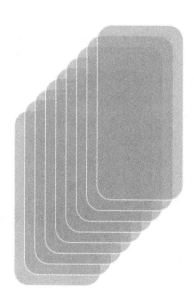

one at any time to indicate if there was something they wanted to speak more about.

The second mechanic we used in this session was breakout groups; we divided the group into smaller murmur groups. The smaller groups allowed for more intimate discussion and they were able to select a representative to report back to the larger group. In this way, everyone's opinion was heard without having to have the whole group listen to each person speak. Because each breakout room had its own digital collaboration space (each breakout room had a link which, when clicked, took the group to another virtual whiteboard), we as facilitators were also able to have a look and see if certain groups were struggling to write something or if they were stuck (see figure 34).

This is an example of the virtual whiteboard each small group saw when they clicked on their links. We had pre-created a template to guide the group's conversation (see figure 35).

We then moved on to a discussion of the project values. We thought it would be one of the most contentious issues, so we had to think carefully about how to present this section. This can be a topic where verbal discussion does not sufficiently surface misalignment. We prepped the architect for this project beforehand to introduce this section and to provide his opinion and choices for the project by moving the sliders. Because we had prepped him and showed him the mechanic (see figure 36), it was easier for the other participants to understand how it worked. Participants seemed to enjoy using the slider to indicate their thoughts without having to immediately explain (see figure 37). This was a low-barrier mechanism for surfacing opinions and visually validating outcomes.

30 mins

Requirements Discussion

We will split into breakout rooms in Zoom and discuss the requirements in our smaller groups. Click on the link below for your group and more instructions will follow:

Breakout Room 1

Breakout Room 2

Breakout Room 3

Breakout Room 4

Breakout Room 5

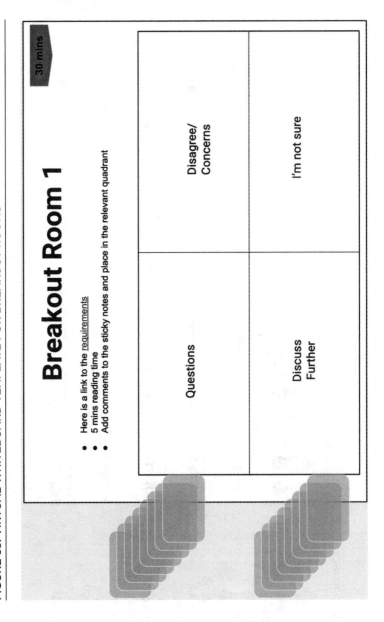

FIGURE 36: PROJECT VALUES SLIDER

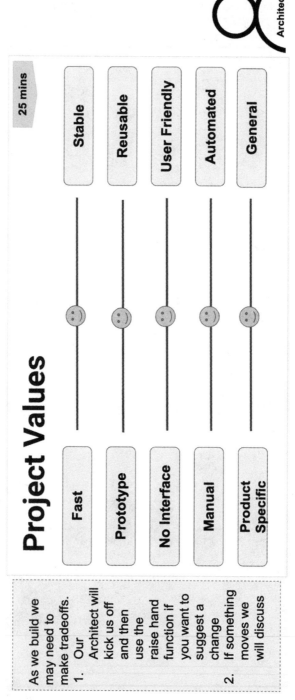

FIGURE 37: PROJECT VALUES SLIDER MOVED BY THE ARCHITECT TO INITIATE THE DISCUSSION

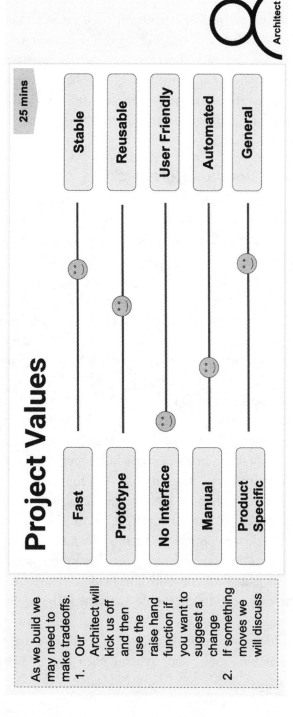

Because so much preparation went into thinking about each individual's experience of the session it went fairly smoothly. Creating spaces where participants could add their thoughts at any time lowered the barrier for contribution. Once this session was over the team was able to use the slide deck as documentation for decision-making going forward.

A WALK THROUGH THE PRINCIPLES

The vehicle you choose for your safari impacts your experience; we hope you never find yourself on a rickety bicycle on such a trip. Similarly, everyone in a remote meeting will have a different experience unless attention is paid to leveling the playing field. This matters because meeting outcomes are affected by the degree to which everyone is able to contribute. If some voices are silenced because they are unable to hear, struggle to understand the language, or experience technical limitations, they are literally excluded. Both individual motivation and meeting quality are sacrificed. How can you **create an equal opportunity** for all to participate in meetings?

Moving from game reserves and into the city, when we think about traffic we think about how things flow and how frustrating it can be to be stopped frequently when driving. The flow and resolution of ideas and conversation in meetings impacts both individual engagement as well as the quality of thinking. Distractions and technical glitches can break flow. Unclear expectations both of the meeting and how to participate in a remote space can make the conversation feel jerky as frequent stops are made to clarify and align. What can you do to **enable the flow** of conversation in meetings?

Building on the image of traffic, road signs are essential sense-making tools. They assist in both guiding behavior as well as reducing cognitive load while driving. Visuals can play a similar role in meetings by making it clear where in the conversation the group is, what is coming next, and reducing the amount of information we need to keep in mind at once. How can you **guide with visuals** in a way the helps the group to grapple with abstract concepts, validate their understandings, and focus on what is important?

Imagine you finally make it out of traffic, maybe thanks to some incredibly well-timed traffic lights, only to get stuck behind a slow driver with no means to overtake them. You might feel frustrated unless you come to understand that person's circumstances. Our ability to understand and connect with another person impacts the way we behave and the way they behave in turn. It can be incredibly difficult to create connection in remote meetings when the space is limited in connection opportunities. However, by paying attention to the human space, you can model behaviors, draw people out, and authentically **nurture connection** within a remote meeting.

Having finally arrived at your destination, the last thing between you and stepping out of the car is a teeny-tiny parking spot, a crowded café, and a flood of anxiety that steadily rises as you struggle and panic. Too much and too little stress have implications for our ability to perform optimally. If people perceive threat in a meeting, the quality of their thinking is compromised. Alternatively, if people are able to engage in playful learning, it is far more likely that constructive, meaningful outcomes will be reached as a result of more engaged, open thinkers. How you set the tone of the meeting, the way you frame questions, the behaviors you model, and the lightness you bring all serve to shift the atmosphere away from threat and toward **playful learning**.

Finally, linking back to the minibus story we began with, imagine jumping in only to realize that this is the first time the driver is driving this vehicle. Do not let your meeting suffer the cost of your inexperience with a tool. Take some time to think about security, access, ease of use, and how to interact with the tool before you put it in front of people. If you can **master your tools,** you are able to focus on the session and the attendees will feel at ease in the hands of a safe driver.

WEAVING TOGETHER THE SCIENCE

The eight "Under the Hood" sections in this book went a little deeper into what is happening behind the scenes when we experience certain things in meetings. **SCARF** is a neuroscientific model for understanding the key domains from which we can interpret threat or reward (things that make us want to move away from or toward something). Each letter represents a domain along which we might perceive threat.

Building on threat detection, we explored what happens in our brains when we experience social pain, such as feeling excluded, and how these experiences activate the same parts of the brain that physical pain does. When experiencing pain our brains are not in optimal problem-solving states. How might we, as facilitators, **create equal opportunity** for people to participate and in so doing, avoid causing people to experience social pain and prevent our meetings from suffering from the effects thereof?

Thinking about things a little more positively, we uncovered what happens when our brains experience "aha" moments and why they feel so good. Our brains are wired to enjoy closing feedback loops and when we do, the chemicals released activate reward networks, which make us want to do more of something. Alternatively, preventing people from closing feedback loops can lead to frustration and disengagement. If you can **enable flow,** you create the conditions in which people can create connections, arrive at insights, and feel good while doing so.

In order to reach an insight, our brains need to hold a certain amount of information in our conscious awareness in order to examine it and make connections. This ability, our working memory, is heavily constrained: we can only recall about four pieces of information without the quality of that information being sacrificed. **Visuals** can be used in a variety of ways to reduce cognitive load in meetings. Visuals can also be incredibly powerful when we consider the role that metaphor plays in deconstructing abstract constructs into relatable pieces as well as in assisting our brains in storing information. If we are able to better comprehend and recall information, meeting conversations and in-turn outcomes will reap the rewards.

Moving on from abstract thought, we returned to the social dynamics of meetings and the neuroscience of social connection. Studies have found that feeling understood and connected activates the same reward circuits described in "aha" moments. Additionally, feeling understood and connected seems to reinforce social behaviors in a self-perpetuating cycle. By **nurturing connection** in a meeting, you create social conditions that support optimal mental performance.

Having explored the impact of positive social interactions, we took a closer look at what happens when we experience stress. The chemicals our brains release when we detect threat have an inverted-U relationship with our ability to engage in higher-order thinking, such as analyzing information or making decisions. Too little stress and our brains kick into holiday mode, too much stress and we can experience stage fright. Alternatively, when our brains are engaged in playful learning, we are able to connect new information in novel, joyful ways. In playful learning there's sufficient activation of the prefrontal cortex to keep us engaged and propel us to keep going. By **enabling playful learning,** your meeting attendees avoid fear-based responses and are able to engage is quality thinking and learning.

Meeting outcomes are affected by the quality of thinking that occurs within them. By avoiding fear and threat-based responses, you give people a chance to think clearly and remain focused. By creating the conditions for ideas to flow, insights to be reached, and playful learning to occur, you not only avoid possibly negative side effects of fear but create the optimal conditions for thinking. Finally, by paying attention to the social aspects of a meeting, you attend to the group dynamics that can inhibit engagement or create and maintain collaborative behavior.

LOOKING AT THE METHODS TOGETHER

We have talked about a lot of mechanics and methods in this book. Any practice is only as powerful as the skill with which it is applied and the appropriateness of it to the given context. These methods can be subtle ways to shift your meetings. If you start with one or two, over time your meetings will evolve into more collaborative spaces. Below is a summary (Table 1); you might notice some techniques that overlap or build on each other.

OUR FINAL ENCOURAGEMENT

Remote meetings can be quite vulnerable spaces for facilitators and participants. We encourage you to experiment and model the behaviors you'd like to see regardless. Face-to-face collaboration will possibly always feel easier, smoother, and more natural. However, as you continue to practice and fine-tune your remote facilitation, you may discover new potential for your teams and organizations in distributed environments. There is always something more to learn and discover and we hope whether it be in your teams, organizations, or communities of practice, that you continue to seek better ways to achieve healthier remote interactions. We hope that by reading this book you now feel a little braver in remote meetings.

TABLE 1: SUMMARIZED TABLE OF PRINCIPLES AND METHODS

Create Equal Opportunity	Enable Flow	Guide with Visuals	Nurture Connection	Enable Playful Learning	Master Your Tools
Go Fully Remote When You Can	Manage Expectations: Make the Agenda Visible	Enrich Information with Visuals	Open the Space with a Check-in Question	Craft Your Container	Start with a Purpose
A "Pseudo Body" as a Substitute	Manage Expectations: Make the Session Rules Visible	Reduce Cognitive Load with Clear Instructions	Work in Smaller Groups	Use Words Wisely	Arrive Prepared
Check Technology in the Beginning	Co-create Visual Documentation	Visualize Remote Space Agreements	Be Intentional about How You Show Up	Use Fun and Meaningful Visuals	Pivot When Necessary
Set up Virtual Stickies	Create Energy Cues	Visually Validate Outcomes	Bring Attention to Differing Contexts	Break the Silence with Music	Back Channels
Lightweight Mechanisms to Display Opinion (e.g., Dot Voting)	Make Space for Breaks		Pay Attention to the Space	Invite a Little Joy	Pair Facilitation
Allow Time for Pre-Reading	Root Participants in the Present		Make It Okay to Leave		Separate Meeting Artifacts from Outcomes
Pre-Populate Names					Consider Access and Security
Pay Attention to the Space					Choosing a Tool
Maintaining Connection When the Call Ends					
Amplify Immediately	Deal with Fallout	Asynchronous Communication	Replicate In-person Interactions	Remote Team Agreements	

NOTES

1. Buffer, "State of Remote Work: How remote workers from around the world feel about remote work, the benefits and struggles that come along with it, and what it's like to be a remote worker in 2019." https://buffer.com/state-of-remote -work-2019# (accessed August 31, 2019).

2. Igloo, "2019 State of the Digital Workplace." http:// igloosoftware.lookbookhq.com/resourcespage/report-igloo -digital?_ga=2.100731971.350767769.1566779246-317818767 .1566779246 (accessed December 10, 2019).

3. Brené Brown, documentary by Sandra Restrepo, *The Call to Courage,* Netflix, April 19, 2019.

4. Brené Brown, *Daring Greatly* (New York: Penguin, 2013), 34.

5. David Rock, "SCARF: a brain-based model for collaborating with and influencing others," *Neuroleadership Journal* no. 1 (2008), http://web.archive.org/web/20100705024057 /http://www.your-brain-at-work.com/files/NLJ_SCARFUS.pdf.

6. David Rock, "SCARF: a brain-based model for collaborating with and influencing others," *Neuroleadership Journal* no. 1 (2008), http://web.archive.org/web/20100705024057/http://www .your-brain-at-work.com/files/NLJ_SCARFUS.pdf.

7. Gerald M. Weinberg, *Becoming a Technical Leader* (Leanpub, 2016), 484.

8. Dr. Jacqui Grey, webinar: *Do We Have Inclusion All Wrong?*, NeuroLeadership Institute. August 13, 2019, https:// hub.neuroleadership.com/include-demo-august-2019?utm _source=hs_email&utm_medium=email&utm_content =75829927&_hsenc=p2ANqtz-_ZtQ759YbIaOhZ0-0PFQnlPN 24grnXkTzYiZCUqYjZDMBYM9_z9nleJIObc9eh3NTuIdNTD ZCPDG3KMMgRCNVkw-x7Uw&_hsmi=75829927 (accessed August 13, 2019).

9. Naomi I. Eisenberger, "Broken Hearts and Broken Bones: A Neural Perspective on the Similarities Between Social and Physical Pain," *Psychosomatic Medicine* 74, no. 2 (2012), https://www.ncbi.nlm.nih.gov/pmc/articles/PMC3273616/.

10. Sam Laing, "Top Tips For Distributed Meetings." Growing Agile, http://www.growingagile.co.nz/2017/06/top -tips-for-distributed-meetings/ (accessed July 15, 2019).

11. Speech. December 3, 1923. Shepherd's Bush Empire, London. (CS IV, 3426.)

12. M. Tik et al., "Ultra-high-field fMRI insights on insight: Neural correlates of the Aha!-moment," *Human Brain Mapping* 39, no. 8 (2018), https://www.ncbi.nlm.nih.gov/pmc/articles /PMC6055807/.

13. Joshua Foer, *Feats of Memory Anyone Can Do*, TED, May 2012, https://www.ted.com/talks/joshua_foer_feats_of _memory_anyone_can_do (accessed June 2019).

14. N. Cowan, "The Magical Mystery Four: How is Working Memory Capacity Limited, and Why?" *Current Directions in Psychological Science* 19, no. 1 (2010), https://www.ncbi.nlm .nih.gov/pmc/articles/PMC2864034/#.

15. GA Miller, "The magical number seven, plus or minus two: Some limits on our capacity for processing information," *Psychological Review* 63 (1956), https://psycnet.apa.org /doiLanding?doi=10.1037%2Fh0043158.

16. N. Cowan, "The Magical Mystery Four: How is Working Memory Capacity Limited, and Why?" *Current Directions in*

Psychological Science 19, no. 1 (2010), https://www.ncbi.nlm.nih.gov/pmc/articles/PMC2864034/#.

17. A. Jamrozik et al., "Metaphor: bridging embodiment to abstraction," *Psychonomic Bulletin & Review* 23, no. 4 (2017), https://www.ncbi.nlm.nih.gov/pmc/articles/PMC5033247/.

18. Joshua Foer, *Moonwalking with Einstein: The Art and Science of Remembering Everything* (New York: The Penguin Group, 2011).

19. Dick Axelrod and Emily Axelrod, *Let's Stop Meeting Like This: Tools to Save Time and Get More Done* (San Francisco: Berrett-Koehler Publishers Inc., 2014), ch. 2.

20. David Rock, "SCARF: a brain-based model for collaborating with and influencing others," *Neuroleadership Journal* no. 1 (2008), http://web.archive.org/web/20100705024057/http://www.your-brain-at-work.com/files/NLJ_SCARFUS.pdf.

21. The Arbinger Institute, *Leadership and Self-Deception: Getting Out of the Box* (California: Berrett-Koehler Publishers, Inc., 2008), 42.

22. S. Morelli et al., "The neural bases of feeling understood and not understood," *Social Cognitive and Affective Neuroscience* 9, no. 12 (2014), https://www.ncbi.nlm.nih.gov/pmc/articles/PMC4249470/.

23. Esther Derby and Diana Larsen, *Agile Retrospectives: Making Good Teams Great* (Texas: Pragmatic Bookshelf, 2006), 5.

24. Harrison Owen, "Open Space for Emerging Order," https://www.openspaceworld.com/brief_history.htm (accessed September 6, 2019).

25. Harrison Owen, "Open Space for Emerging Order," https://www.openspaceworld.com/brief_history.htm (accessed September 6, 2019).

26. Diane Ackerman, *Deep Play* (Vintage, 1999), 11.

27. Amy F. T. Arnsten, "Stress signalling pathways that impair prefrontal cortex structure and function," *Nature Reviews Neuroscience*, 10, no. 6 (2009), https://www.ncbi.nlm.nih.gov/pmc/articles/PMC2907136/.

28. David Rock, *Your Brain at Work: Strategies for Overcoming Distraction, Regaining Focus, and Working Smarter All Day Long* (New York: Harper Collins, 2009).

29. David Rock, *Your Brain at Work: Strategies for Overcoming Distraction, Regaining Focus, and Working Smarter All Day Long* (New York: Harper Collins, 2009).

30. Amy F. T. Arnsten, "Stress signalling pathways that impair prefrontal cortex structure and function," *Nature Reviews Neuroscience* 10, no. 6 (2009), https://www.ncbi.nlm.nih.gov/pmc/articles/PMC2907136/.

31. Claire Liu et al., "Neuroscience and learning through play: a review of the evidence" (research summary), *The LEGO Foundation* (2017), https://www.legofoundation.com/media/1064/neuroscience-review_web.pdf.

32. Claire Liu et al., "Neuroscience and learning through play: a review of the evidence" (research summary), *The LEGO Foundation* (2017), https://www.legofoundation.com/media/1064/neuroscience-review_web.pdf.

33. Claire Liu et al., "Neuroscience and learning through play: a review of the evidence" (research summary), *The LEGO Foundation* (2017), https://www.legofoundation.com/media/1064/neuroscience-review_web.pdf.

34. The X-Team, The Definitive Guide to Remote Development Teams: https://x-team.com/remote-team-guide/communication/ (accessed November 21, 2019).

35. The Scrum Guide: https://www.scrum.org/resources/scrum-guide (accessed November 10, 2019).

ACKNOWLEDGMENTS

First and foremost this book would not even exist if it were not for Esther Derby. We have immense gratitude to her for connecting us to our editor, Charlotte Ashlock. To Charlotte, we'd like to say thank you for your guidance, wisdom, and patience over the past year and a half. To Valerie Caldwell, thank you so much for understanding our vision and ideas for this book. We'd also like to thank you for finding the perfect illustrator, Yvonne Chan, who captured the book cover so beautifully.

We'd like to thank our reviewers—Cara Turner, Dick Axelrod, and Douglas Hammer—for taking the time to give us honest and meaningful feedback. We learned something from each of you which we will take with us beyond the bounds of this book. An extra special thank-you to Cara for being one of the people who has shaped a lot of how we see facilitation and neuroscience applied to the workspace. We treasure you.

To Louise Perold and Kevin Trethaway, thank you for inspiring us to write a book independent of this opportunity. Your belief in us could not go unrecognized. You are two incredibly inspiring humans who have taught us so much from the examples that you lead.

We'd also like to thank Jo Perold, Antoinette Coetzee, Steve Holyer, Sam Laing, Karen Greaves, Austin Fagan, Justin Kotze, Kaluhi Anzigale, Bee Sharwood, Willy Bogonko, Aveshan Govender, Ted Pietrzak, and Mark Kilby for being wonderful support systems in our lives. You have each in your own way inspired us to continuously grow and been foundational in shaping how we approach facilitation and teams. It would be almost impossible to quantify the impact you have had on our lives.

We'd like to thank the SUGSA (Scrum User Group of South Africa) community and the Hacking Remote Facilitation group for allowing us to learn, experiment, grow, and receive feedback.

Thank you to the incredible teams who have walked this journey along the way. In particular, we'd like to thank Ninjas, Team X, GoG, CD5, and WTF—you have had an impact on our lives for which we will forever be grateful.

We'd especially like to thank our families who love us despite the messy bits they get to see.

From Kirsten: Thank you to Anita, Shaun, and Shannon. Your unconditional love and support gives me the courage to take on crazy things like writing a book. I would not be who I am without you.

From Jay-Allen: Thank you to Jacqui, Ashley, Roxanne, Caleb, and Granny B for providing the space for me to chase whatever challenges I face. I love you all and you are such special humans.

Lastly, a huge thank-you to our partners Nelson Nogueira and Wesley De Wet. We thank you for your love and unwavering belief that we can do anything, and your patience when we had lots of work (not to mention your cooking and cleaning skills when our noses were in research papers). We are incredibly lucky and we love you.

INDEX

Note: Page numbers followed by *f* indicate a figure on the corresponding page.

access concerns, 112, 114,
Ackerman, Diane, 90
active engagement and playful learning, 93, 95
after the call: amplification and reiteration, 116–117; asynchronous communication, 117–119; fallout concerns, 117; introduction, 115; maintaining connection, 120–121; remote team agreements, 120; replication of in-person interactions, 119–120
agendas, 21–22, 51, 52*f*
Agile frameworks, 6
Aha!-moments, 49
alternative communication, 9

amplification after the call, 116–117, 121
anterior singular cortex, 30
Arbinger Institute, 78
asynchronous communication, 117–119
attention to different contexts, 85–87, 86*f*
autonomy: direct threat to, 16; of facilitators, 15; of individuals, 16; in mobile technology development team, 17, 18; in SCARF, 12
awareness in meetings, 1, 16, 19, 85, 86*f*, 87, 119, 143
Axelrod, Dick, 77
Axelrod, Emily, 77

back channels, 70 , 88, 100,
108, 114
behavioral cues, 49, 56
body-language cues, 23, 32, 66
brain function: memory capacity,
64; neural correlates, 49;
physical pain, 30–31; playful
learning, 90–96; prefrontal
cortex, 92–93; reducing
cognitive load, 66–68
breaks in meetings, 56–58,
54f–55f, 57f–58f, 61
Brown, Brené, 7

certainty in SCARF, 11–12, 19
check-in questions, 81–83,
97, 125f
Churchill, Winston, 48
co-creation of visual documentation, 53, 61
Coetzee, Antoinette, 24
cognitive functioning, 30, 63, 92
cognitive load, 66–68
collaboration tools, 25, 112–113.
See also remote collaboration
co-location meetings: equal
opportunity creation, 32;
guerilla facilitation, 24;
mastering tools for, 106–107;
meeting artifacts *vs.* outcomes,
109, 110f, 111f; teams in,
8–13, 122–133, 124f–126f,
128f–132f; tying it together,
122–133, 124f–126f,
128f–132f
color-coding information, 66
communication: alternative
communication, 9; asynchronous communication,
117–119; extra effort, 12,
19; over-communication,
118; synchronous communi-
cation, 117–118; verbal

communication, 9, 12, 19,
122, 133; visual communication, 133
communication challenges 9–10,
107, 117–119, 133
conferencing tools, 113
connectedness, needs, 12
connections. *See* personal
connections
conscious decisions, 62, 63
container creation for attendees,
103
creative solutions, 32
cultural norms/nuances, 17–19

decision-making documentation,
140
Derby, Esther, 81
digital sticky notes, 35–38,
36f–37f, 107
disengagement in meetings, 50
distraction in meetings, 50, 59
diversity considerations, 50,
133
dopamine, 92, 94
du Maurier, Daphne, 105
dysfunction after the call, 121

email follow-up, 116
enabling flow of conversations,
140, 143
energy cues and breaks, 56–58,
54f–55f, 57f–58f, 61
"energy gauge" symbol, 53
engagement in meetings, 25, 33,
51
enriching information with visual
cues, 65–66, 67f, 75
equal opportunity creation:
brain function and physical
pain, 30–31; group opinion
displays, 38–41, 39f–40f;
introduction to, 28–31;

methods and mechanics,
32–33, 47; for participants,
140, 142; pre-populating
names, 41–43, 42f; pre-
reading time, 41; "pseudo
body" substitute, 33–34;
remote meeting types, 31–32;
space considerations, 43–46,
44f–45f; summary of, 46–47;
technology considerations,
34–35, 46; virtual stickies,
35–38, 36f–37f
expectation management, 51, 52f,
61, 81–83
external service providers, 17

face-to-face conversations, 29
fairness concerns, 12–13, 15, 17, 19
fallout concerns, 117
familiarity concerns, 18, 19
fear: detrimental effects of, 94;
isolation and, 14; in mobile
technology development team,
19; remote collaboration,
10–13; survival-based decision
making, 91
flow of meetings: Aha!-moments,
49; co-creation of visual
documentation, 53, 61;
enabling of, 59–61, 60f; energy
cues and breaks, 56–58,
54f–55f, 57f–58f; introduction
to, 48–51; managing expectations, 51, 52f, 61; methods and
mechanics, 51, 52f; rooting
participants in the present,
59, 61
Foer, Joshua, 61
friction during meetings, 117
frustration in meetings, 50
fully remote meetings, 32,
133–135, 136f–139f, 140
fun after the call, 121

global financial technology
firm, 13
Google Slides, 59, 112
Grey, Jacqui, 28
groups: guerilla facilitation,
24; norms of, 9, 12, 19;
opinion displays, 38–41,
39f–40f; problem-solving
ability, 23–24; size considerations, 25; status in, 15;
working in smaller groups,
83–84
guerilla facilitation, 24–25
guiding visuals, 72–75, 141

higher-order thinking, 143
higher-quality participation, 91
humor usage, 103
hybrid remoting, 32

idea creation, 35
information management, 65–66,
67f, 72
"in-meeting" strategies, 80–81
in-person facilitation: experiences
of, 32; interactions, 119–120;
introduction to, 3, 5; success
of, 8
instructional clarity, 72
intended purpose, 106–107
intention of facilitators, 84–85
in-the-moment decisions, 85, 87
invisible group norms, 9, 12
isolation and fear, 14
iteration and playful learning,
93, 95

joy and playful learning, 93, 94,
102–103

Laing, Sam, 32
language barriers, 17, 19, 46
language use, 97–98

Larsen, Diana, 81
Law of Two Feet or the Law of Mobility, 87–88
Leadership and Self-Deception (Arbinger Institute), 78
leaving meetings, 87–88
LEGO Foundation, 94
linear sequence text, 35
low-barrier mechanism, 140

managing expectations. *See* expectation management
mastering tools. *See* tool mastery in remote meetings
meaning and playful learning, 93, 95
meaningful visuals, 98, 99*f*
meeting artifacts *vs.* outcomes, 109, 110*f*, 111*f*
meeting phases, 21–22
memory/memory capacity: brain function, 63; survival-based decision making, 91; working memory, 63, 65, 70, 92, 143
messaging follow-up, 116
Microsoft's PowerPoint, 112
mindset-shifting, 34
misunderstandings/misinterpretations, 71
mobile technology development team, 16–18
multiple-location offices, 2
multitasking, 14–15, 19
music use, 100–102, 101*f*, 103, 119

neural correlates, 49
neuroscience: of remote facilitation, 5–6, 10–13; of social connection, 79–80; stressful feelings and, 92–93

noradrenaline, 92
nurture connection, 141, 145

observation in guerilla facilitation, 24–25
observation of others, 15–16
Open Space rule, 87–88
outcome-focused conversations, 95
outcomes *vs.* meeting artifacts, 109, 110*f*, 111*f*
over-communication, 118
overcontrolling the space, 23
Owen, Harrison, 87–88

pair facilitation and mastering tools, 108
participant anxiety, 43
personal connections: attention to different contexts, 85–87, 86*f*; check-in questions, 81–83; intention of facilitators, 84–85; introduction to, 77–81; leaving meetings, 87–88; methods and mechanics, 81–83; nurturing of, 88–89; working in smaller groups, 83–84
perspectives at hand, 72
physical pain and brain function, 30–31
playful learning: defined, 94–95; enabling of, 103–104, 141; introduction to, 90–96; joy and, 93, 94, 102–103; language use, 97–98; meaningful visuals, 98, 99*f*; methods and mechanics, 96–97, 141, 144; music use, 100–102, 101*f*, 103; stressful feelings, 92–93
power: distribution mechanisms, 133; imbalances of, 32; of remote facilitators, 15

prefrontal cortex, 92
preparation and mastering tools,
    107–108, 114
pre-populating names, 41–43, 42*f*
pre-reading time, 41
presentation tools, 113
principles-based approach, 4
problem-solving, 23–24, 29
provider-related Internet issues,
    133
"pseudo body" substitute, 33–34

quality meetings, 21–22
quality thinking, 103

"raise hand" mechanism, 9
real-time collaboration, 107
recall of concepts, 72
regional skills scarcity, 2
reiteration after the call, 116–117
relatedness concept, 12, 14,
    17, 19
remote collaboration: co-location
    teams, 8–13; fears over, 10–13;
    introduction to, 7–8; in
    meetings, 25; mobile technol-
    ogy development team, 16–18;
    neuroscience and, 5–6, 10–13;
    in organizations, 2; reasons for
    difficulties, 18–19
remote facilitation: guerilla
    facilitation, 24–25; importance
    of, 2–3; introduction to, 1–2;
    during meeting, 22; neurosci-
    ence of, 5–6, 9–11; prior to
    start of meeting, 21–22;
    purpose of, 113; summary of,
    27; theoretical concepts, 4–5;
    types of meetings, 25, 26*f*,
    31–32, 46; value of, 3
remote facilitators: intention
    of, 84–85; meeting phases,

21–22, 22*f*; power of, 15;
    problem-solving ability
    of groups, 23–24; role of,
    20–21
remote meeting types, 25, 26*f*,
    31–32, 46
remote space agreements, 68–70,
    71
remote team agreements, 120
replication of in-person interac-
    tions, 119–120
reporting-style behavior, 13–14
reward circuitry, 94
Rock, David, 10–11
rooting participants in the
    present, 59, 61
"rule of the space," 21

SCARF model, 10–11, 78, 142
security concerns, 112
sense-making tool, 64
session requirements/rules, 51,
    61, 107
social behavior, 5–6, 10–13
social cognition models, 9
social connection, 79–80, 102
social interactions, 9, 93, 95
social pain, 31, 79, 142
social psychology, 4, 6
solo remoting, 31
South African minibus taxis,
    20–21
space considerations for meetings,
    43–46, 44*f*–45*f*
Sprint Reviews, 123, 126*f*
status: in groups, 15; reporting
    on, 13; in SCARF, 10–11
stressful feelings, 92–93
survival-based decision making,
    91
synchronous communication,
    117–118

team-related activities, 120
team/teams: autonomy in mobile technology development, 17, 18; coaching methods, 6; co-located teams, 8–13, 122–133, 124*f*–126*f*, 128*f*–132*f*; motivation of, 31; remote team agreements, 120
technical barriers, 9–10, 19, 51
technology considerations: equal opportunity creation, 34–35, 46; fears, 19; global financial technology firm, 13; mobile technology development team, 16–18
thinking styles, 46
timeboxes (time limits), 50, 51, 127
time zone differences, 18, 117
tiredness in meetings, 50
tool mastery in remote meetings: access and security, 112; back channels and, 108; choosing tools, 112–113; direction changes, 108; intended purpose, 106–107; introduction to, 105–106; meeting artifacts *vs.* outcomes, 109, 110*f*, 111*f*; overview of, 113–114, 142; pair facilitation and, 108; preparation and, 107–108, 114
trust by default, 118
Turner, Cara, 24
tying it together: co-located teams, 8–13, 122–133, 123*f*–126*f*, 128*f*–132*f*; fully remote meetings, 133–135, 136*f*–139*f*

uncertainty in remote meetings, 7–8, 14–16, 18, 23, 68, 91
unconscious decisions, 62
understanding of outcomes, 72

validating outcomes with visual cues, 70–72, 73*f*
verbal communication, 9, 12, 19, 122, 133
video-conferencing chats, 35
virtual game sessions, 120
virtual stickies, 35–38, 36*f*–37*f*, 107
visual communication, 133
visual cues: enriching information with, 65–66, 67*f*, 70; guides for, 73–76; introduction to, 62–65; metaphors and abstract thought, 74–75; methods and mechanics, 65–66, 144; as playful learning, 103; reducing cognitive load, 66–68, 69*f*; remote space agreements, 68–70, 71*f*; validating outcomes with, 70–72, 73*f*
visual documentation, 53
vulnerability meetings, 7, 13–16, 84

watercooler talk, 119
Weinberg, Gerald M., 20
working in smaller groups, 83–84
working memory, 63, 65, 70, 92, 143
work-life balance, 2
writing mechanisms, 123, 127

ABOUT THE AUTHORS

Kirsten Clacey (left) and Jay-Allen Morris (right).
Photo by Aletta Francina.

Kirsten Clacey and **Jay-Allen Morris** offer remote facilitation training and consulting services to companies across the world. They have specialized in enabling distributed teams to reach high performance, using a combination of adapted facilitation techniques, team coaching methods, and Agile frameworks. They have spoken and continue to speak at conferences on the topic of remote facilitation and creating effective distributed spaces. They have also worked together to create an online video course on remote facilitation.

Both Kirsten and Jay-Allen work as Team Coaches in the Agile space. Over the course of their careers, they have held the roles of Agile Lead, Agile Facilitator, Scrum Master, and Team Coach. They have worked with a range of companies, from large, established organizations to small startups.

Kirsten has an educational background in clinical and neuropsychology. She has built on her psychology background in her work with software teams. She has focused primarily on the financial technology sector, working with both local and distributed teams. From 2016–2019, Kirsten served her local Agile community by being on the SUGSA Committee (Scrum User Group of South Africa), organizing monthly Meetups and the Regional Scrum Gathering in SA.

Jay-Allen has a background in humanities, which has been invaluable in her various roles within the tech industry. She found it natural to transition into the role of Team Coach. She has been focusing on creating effective team spaces, both in person and remote. She volunteered for the SUGSA Committee from 2017–2018, organizing the annual conference and encouraging new speakers.

Find out more about us at https://theremotecoaches.com/

Dear reader,

Thank you for picking up this book and welcome to the worldwide BK community! You're joining a special group of people who have come together to create positive change in their lives, organizations, and communities.

What's BK all about?

Our mission is to connect people and ideas to create a world that works for all.

Why? Our communities, organizations, and lives get bogged down by old paradigms of self-interest, exclusion, hierarchy, and privilege. But we believe that can change. That's why we seek the leading experts on these challenges—and share their actionable ideas with you.

A welcome gift

To help you get started, we'd like to offer you a **free copy** of one of our bestselling ebooks:

www.bkconnection.com/welcome

When you claim your **free ebook**, you'll also be subscribed to our blog.

Our freshest insights

Access the best new tools and ideas for leaders at all levels on our blog at ideas.bkconnection.com.

Sincerely,

Your friends at Berrett-Koehler

MIX
Paper from
responsible sources
FSC® C008955

Certified

Corporation